R.I.P.

Here Lie the Famous Last Words,
Epitaphs, Morbid Musings,
and Fond Farewells of the Famous
and Not-So-Famous

Edited by Susan K. Hom

STERLING

New York / London
www.sterlingpublishing.com

For my parents and my sister, Jamie, with love

STERLING and the distinctive Sterling logo are registered trademarks
of Sterling Publishing Co., Inc.

Library of Congress Cataloging-in-Publication Data

RIP : famous last words, epitaphs, morbid musings, and fond farewells
of the famous and not-so-famous / edited by Susan K. Hom.
— p. cm.
ISBN-13: 978-1-4027-4683-3
ISBN-10: 1-4027-4683-0
1. Last words. 2. Epitaphs. 3. Death—Quotations, maxims, etc. I. Hom, Susan K.
PN6328.L3R57 2007
082—dc22   2006033791

10 9 8 7 6 5 4 3 2 1

Published by Sterling Publishing Co., Inc.
387 Park Avenue South, New York, NY 10016
© 2007 by Sterling Publishing Co., Inc.
Distributed in Canada by Sterling Publishing
c/o Canadian Manda Group, 165 Dufferin Street
Toronto, Ontario, Canada M6K 3H6
Distributed in the United Kingdom by GMC Distribution Services
Castle Place, 166 High Street, Lewes, East Sussex, England BN7 1XU
Distributed in Australia by Capricorn Link (Australia) Pty. Ltd.
P.O. Box 704, Windsor, NSW 2756, Australia

Interior design by Bob Steimle
Cover design by Glenn Gustafson

Printed in China
All rights reserved

Sterling ISBN-13: 978-1-4027-4683-3
ISBN-10: 1-4027-4683-0

For information about custom editions, special sales, premium and
corporate purchases, please contact Sterling Special Sales
Department at 800-805-5489 or specialsales@sterlingpub.com.

CONTENTS

Introduction: A Cordial Invitation 5

🌿

Epitaphs: Wit and Wisdom from the Cemetery 7

✳

Musings: Poking Fun at Death 67

♣

Farewells: Last Words to Die By 113

⊕

Index 156

Introduction:
A Cordial Invitation

You're invited to a reunion party. It's a host of ghosts! Gathered in these pages are some of the most famous and infamous people the world has ever known, including George Washington, Bette Davis, John Wilkes Booth, and Al Capone. These colorful personalities give their two cents about death, and their family and friends (and enemies) left on this side of the light also have a few things to say about their passing. You'll meet world leaders, criminals, scientists, actors, musicians, and writers from all walks of life. It's quite a gathering!

The first chapter offers the most interesting epitaphs of all time. These graveyard literary gems are from dozens of cemeteries found in the United States and Europe. They're from the headstones of ordinary people, celebrities, and even animals. This section has humorous rhymes with plenty of puns, moving tributes, and heartfelt good-byes.

The second chapter is packed with amusing quotations about death. They're clever, cynical, and just plain funny. Everything is covered—including cemeteries, funerals, and undertakers!

The third chapter features memorable last words. Some people were ready to go, while others would have loved to stick around. Some people were busy up until the last moment, and others savored the natural beauty around them. These last words are candid and thoughtful. It's a rare look at celebrities' (and regular folks') most private moments.

The distinguished guests are eager to get started. Some of them have been lying around for hundreds of years. Now it's their turn to have the final say.

Epitaphs: Wit and Wisdom from the Cemetery

I t's time to take a look at the granite yearbook pages of celebrities and ordinary folk from years gone by. Just like a high school yearbook, tombstones have profound statements about life, clever jokes, and sentimental good-byes from family and friends. The only difference is that these words are permanent—truly etched in stone. It's too bad that some stonecutters didn't spell-check their work. The omission of one letter makes all the difference. Just ask Susannah Ensign, whose tombstone reads, "Lord, I am Thin." Oops!

The best part about ancient tombstones is their hilariously clever rhymes. Okay, some of the rhymes are a little forced and over the top, but that adds to the charm. Consider this one: "Underneath this ancient pew / Lie the remains of Jonathan Blue; / His name was Black, but that wouldn't do." The author actually changed the name of the deceased to accommodate his rhyme. Poor Jonathan!

Some epitaphs are written by the deceased before their demise; but most of them are created by colleagues and family. So be kind to your friends, or you may get one very lame tombstone inscription, which the whole world will remember you by.

Last but not least, this chapter has tombstone inscriptions of beloved celebrities. In these pages, you'll find well-known actors, political leaders, scientists, artists, and writers—everyone from Thomas Jefferson to Cary Grant. So take your time and wander through the pages of this virtual cemetery.

Performing Artists

The Best Is Yet to Come
Beloved Husband & Father
—Frank Sinatra
SINGER

*

Vanity Fair *suggested this epitaph for actor W. C. Fields:*
ON THE WHOLE, I'D RATHER
BE IN PHILADELPHIA.

*

"And the angels sing"
–Johnny Mercer
SINGER

*

Playwright & Poet
His foe was folly
& his weapon wit.
–W. S. Gilbert
LIBRETTIST

Film director Alfred Hitchcock suggested this epitaph for himself:

I'M INVOLVED IN A PLOT.

✳

This inscription is on a memorial piece near the graves of musicians Johnny Cash and June Carter Cash:

(front)
Cash—Carter
I Walk the Line

Wildwood Flower

(back)
2003
Happiness is being at peace;
being with loved ones;
being comfortable. . . .
But most of all,
it's having those loved ones.
Johnny Cash

✳

BALLET MASTER
–George Balanchine
CHOREOGRAPHER

BELOVED WIFE
BILLIE
HOLIDAY
KNOWN AS
"LADY DAY"
—Billie Holiday
SINGER

✳

Singer/actor Bing Crosby suggested this epitaph for himself:

HE WAS AN
AVERAGE GUY
WHO COULD
CARRY A TUNE.

✳

EXIT BURBAGE.
—Richard Burbage
ACTOR

The most excellent
Musician
Any Age has produced;
Whose compositions were a
Sentimental Language
Rather than mere Sounds;
And surpassed the Power of
Words in expressing
The various Passions
Of the Human Heart.
–George Frederick Handel
COMPOSER

*

Actor Jack Benny suggested this epitaph for himself:
DID YOU HEAR ABOUT MY OPERATION?

*

FOREVER IN OUR HEARTS
–Jimi Hendrix
MUSICIAN

AND THE BEAT GOES ON
–Sonny Bono
SINGER

✳

This plaque at Symphony Hall in Boston, Massachusetts, is dedicated to William Henry Hartley, bandmaster, and the musicians of the S.S. Titanic:

In Memory of
The Devoted Musicians
Wallace Henry Hartley, Bandmaster
John Frederick Preston Clark
Percy Cornelius Taylor
John Wesley Woodward
W. Theodore Brailey
John Law Hume
George Krins
Roger Bricoux

WHO WERE DROWNED

STILL PLAYING

AS THE TITANIC WENT DOWN

APRIL 15, 1912.

"For He shall give His angels charge
over thee to keep thee in all thy ways"
–Jimmy Stewart
ACTOR

*

*Lyricist Howard Ashman—who wrote the lyrics for Disney's
animated films* The Little Mermaid, Beauty and the Beast, *and*
Aladdin*—has the following epitaph:*
O, THAT HE HAD ONE MORE
SONG TO SING.

*

Actor Louise Brooks suggested this epitaph for herself:
I NEVER GAVE AWAY ANYTHING
WITHOUT WISHING I HAD
KEPT IT; NOR KEPT ANYTHING
WITHOUT WISHING I HAD
GIVEN IT AWAY.

*

Television host Johnny Carson suggested this epitaph for himself:
I'LL BE RIGHT BACK.

I WILL ALWAYS LOVE YOU
MY DARLING
THANK YOU
–Fred Astaire
DANCER

*

One of America's legendary entertainers,
whose career spanned more than a half century
crossing all international borders.
Equally at home before the royalty of Europe
and the farm folk of Midwestern USA.
A performer whose unique style adapted to all media
Literary, Radio, Movies, Recordings, Night Clubs,
Broadway and Concert Stage.
Carl Sandburg called him
"The mightiest ballad singer
of this or any other century."
He lives on through his art.
–Burl Ives
SINGER

Tomorrow is the most important thing in life.
Comes into us at midnight very clean.
It's perfect when it arrives and it puts itself into our hands.
It hopes we've learned something from yesterday.

–John Wayne

ACTOR

*

IN LOVING MEMORY OF
VIVIEN LEIGH

. . . NOW BOAST THEE, DEATH,
IN THY POSSESSION LIES
A LASS UNPARALLEL'D . . .

–Vivien Leigh

ACTOR

*

"DUKE"
EDWARD KENNEDY ELLINGTON
–Duke Ellington
COMPOSER

The Heart and Voice of an Angel
The World is a Far Lesser Place Without You
–Carl Dean Wilson
MUSICIAN

✳

There goes the neighborhood.
–Rodney Dangerfield
COMEDIAN AND ACTOR

✳

A Genius of Comedy
His talent brought joy and
laughter to all the world.
–Oliver Hardy
ACTOR

✳

We live to love you more each day.
–Jayne Mansfield
ACTOR

Businessman Ted Turner had this suggestion for his epitaph:
DO NOT DISTURB.

*

THE LAST STOOGE
–Joe DeRita
ACTOR

*

Keep a song in your heart
–Lawrence Welk
MUSICIAN

*

Actor Hedy Lamarr suggested this epitaph for herself:
THIS IS TOO DEEP FOR ME.

*

Actor Gloria Swanson wanted her epitaph to read:
SHE PAID THE BILLS. THAT'S THE STORY OF MY PRIVATE LIFE.

"The Entertainer"
He did it all
Your loving wife Altovise and
father of Tracey, Mark, Jeff, Manny
–Sammy Davis Jr.
ACTOR

*

Actor Michael Caine suggested this epitaph for himself:
BEEN THERE, DONE THAT.

*

A Master of Comedy
His genius in the art of
humor brought gladness
to the world he loved.
–Stan Laurel
ACTOR

*

Someone in Hollywood once suggested this epitaph for actor John Garfield:
DIED IN THE SADDLE.

Actor Cary Grant suggested this epitaph for himself:
HE WAS LUCKY,
AND HE KNEW IT.

*

FOREVER IN OUR HEARTS
–Dinah Shore
SINGER

*

EVERYBODY LOVES SOMEBODY SOMETIME
–Dean Martin
SINGER

*

Beloved Father • Devoted Son

Peace At Last
–Lenny Bruce
COMEDIAN

THE ARTIST MUST ELECT TO FIGHT FOR FREEDOM OR SLAVERY. I HAVE MADE MY CHOICE. I HAD NO ALTERNATIVE.

–Paul Robeson

ACTOR

*

"SATCHMO" LOUIS ARMSTRONG

–Louis Armstrong

MUSICIAN

*

Actor Lionel Barrymore suggested this epitaph for himself:

WELL, I'VE PLAYED EVERYTHING BUT A HARP.

BELOVED MOTHER
TO YESTERDAY'S
COMPANIONSHIP AND
TOMORROW'S REUNION
–Rita Hayworth
ACTOR

*

SHE DID IT THE HARD WAY
–Bette Davis
ACTOR

*

GOOD-NIGHT, SWEET PRINCE,
AND FLIGHTS OF ANGELS SING THEE
TO THY REST.
–Douglas Fairbanks
ACTOR

A STAR ON EARTH–A STAR IN HEAVEN
–Karen Carpenter
SINGER

*

"TOMMY"
THE SENTIMENTAL GENTLEMAN
–Thomas Dorsey Jr.
BIG BAND LEADER

*

Comedienne—Ballerina
–Gilda Radner
ACTOR

*

"Sheltered Love"
–Liberace
MUSICIAN

AT LAST I GET TOP BILLING.
–Wallace Ford
ACTOR

✳

Actor George Jessel suggested this epitaph for himself:
I TELL YOU HERE FROM THE SHADE
IT IS ALL WORTHWHILE.

✳

Together again.
–Gracie Allen and George Burns
ACTORS

✳

*Actor Mel Blanc was the voice of many cartoon characters
including Bugs Bunny, Daffy Duck, and Porky Pig,
and his epitaph reads:*
"THAT'S ALL FOLKS"
MAN OF 1000 VOICES
BELOVED HUSBAND AND FATHER

There's Nothing Nice to Say

Here lies the body of Richard Hind,
Who was neither ingenious, sober, nor kind.
–Richard Hind

*

UNDER THIS SOD LIES ANOTHER ONE.
–Anonymous

*

JOHN BURNS.
–John (no last name)

*

*Writer Robert Benchley suggested this epitaph for
an actress who had a sordid love life:*
SHE SLEEPS ALONE AT LAST.

To the memory of Mary Gold,
Who was gold in nothing but her name,
She was a tolerable woman for an acquaintance
But old Harry himself couldn't live with her.
Her temper was furious
Her tongue was vindictive
She resented a look and frowned at a smile,
And was sour as vinegar.
She punished the earth upwards of 40 years,
To say nothing of her relations.
—Mary Gold

*

Beneath this stone lies Johnnie Scott.
Who lived like a fool and died like a sot,
But it is needless to argue
Whether he was so or not;
He as a man was despised,
And will soon be forgot.
—Johnnie Scott

POORLY LIVED
AND POORLY DIED
POORLY BURIED
AND NO ONE CRIED.
—Anonymous

✳

HE WAS.
—Richard Groombridge

✳

DEEPLY REGRETTED
BY ALL WHO
NEVER KNEW HIM.
—Anonymous

Famous Leaders and Historical Figures

Here was buried
Thomas Jefferson
Author of the
Declaration
of
American Independence
of the
Statute of Virginia
for
Religious Freedom
and Father of the
University of Virginia.
Born April 2, 1743 O.S.
Died July 4, 1826
–Thomas Jefferson
U.S. PRESIDENT

"IF I TAKE THE WINGS OF THE MORNING, AND DWELL IN THE UTTERMOST PARTS OF THE SEA."
–Charles Lindbergh
AVIATOR

*

Mother of the Modern Day
Civil Rights Movement
–Rosa Parks
CIVIL RIGHTS ACTIVIST

*

His fame is his best epitaph.
–Patrick Henry
POLITICAL LEADER OF THE AMERICAN REVOLUTION

*

Here a mound suffices for
one for whom the world
was not large enough.
Sufficit huic tumulus
Cui non sufficeret obis.
–Alexander the Great
KING OF MACEDON

MY JESUS MERCY.
—Al Capone
GANGSTER

✳

Cartoonist Nicolas Bentley suggested this mock epitaph
for Prime Minister Henry Campbell-Bannerman:
HE IS REMEMBERED CHIEFLY AS THE MAN ABOUT WHOM ALL IS FORGOTTEN.

✳

WORKERS OF ALL LANDS UNITE.
THE PHILOSOPHERS HAVE ONLY INTERPRETED THE WORLD IN VARIOUS WAYS, THE POINT HOWEVER IS TO CHANGE IT.
—Karl Marx
PHILOSOPHER

*This inscription is on a monument honoring the first U.S. Secretary
of the Treasury, Alexander Hamilton:*
To the memory of
Alexander Hamilton
The Corporation of Trinity Church has erected this
Monument
In testimony of their Respect
For
The Patriot of incorruptible Integrity,
The Soldier of approved Valour,
The Statesman of consummate Wisdom;
Whose talents and Virtues will be admired
By
Grateful Posterity
Long after this Marble shall have moulded into Dust
He died July 2nd, 1804, Aged 47.

*

LA-ZI-YAH
APACHE
WARRIOR
WITH
GERONIMO
–La-Zi-Yah

NATIVE AMERICAN WARRIOR

Here Lies Buried
Samuel Adams
Signer of the Declaration of Independence
Governor of this Commonwealth
A Leader of Men and an ardent Patriot
—Samuel Adams
POLITICAL LEADER OF THE AMERICAN REVOLUTION

*

MISSION
SPECIALIST
SPACE
SHUTTLE
COLUMBIA
CAPT.
US NAVY
—David McDowell Brown
ASTRONAUT

*

Poet E. E. Cummings suggested this mock epitaph for
U.S. President Warren G. Harding:
The only man, woman or child who wrote a simple declarative
sentence with seven grammatical errors is dead.

British Liaison Officer T. E. Lawrence was also known as "Lawrence of Arabia":

To the dear memory of
T. E. Lawrence
Fellow of All Souls College
Oxford
Born 19 August 1888
Died 19 May 1935
The hour is coming & now is
when the dead shall hear
the voice of the
Son of God
and they that hear
shall live.

*

" . . . THAT NOTHING'S SO
SACRED AS HONOR,
AND NOTHING SO LOYAL
AS LOVE!"
–**Wyatt Earp**
GUNFIGHTER

Mary,
widow of Elder Cushman
and daughter of Isaac Allerton,
Died XXVII November, MDCXIX
Aged about XC years
The last survivor of the first comers
In the Mayflower.
—Mary Cushman

*

Here lies Fred,
Who was alive and is dead;
Had it been his father,
I had much rather;
Had it been his brother,
Still better than another;
Had it been his sister,
No one would have missed her;
Had it been the whole generation,
Still better for the nation:
But since 'tis only Fred,
Who was alive and is dead,—
There's no more to be said.
—Frederick
PRINCE OF WALES

Politician George W. Plunkitt once said "If my worst enemy was given the job
of writing my epitaph when I'm gone, he couldn't do more than write":

GEORGE W. PLUNKITT. HE SEEN HIS
OPPORTUNITIES AND HE TOOK 'EM.

*

The inscription on the Lincoln Memorial is by Royal Cortissoz,
an art critic of the New York Herald Tribune:

IN THIS TEMPLE
AS IN THE HEARTS OF THE PEOPLE
FOR WHOM HE SAVED THE UNION
THE MEMORY OF
ABRAHAM
LINCOLN
IS ENSHRINED FOREVER.

*

"And now abide Faith, Hope,
Love, These Three; but the
greatest of these is Love."
1 Corinthians 13:13
–Coretta Scott King
CIVIL RIGHTS ACTIVIST

U.S. Vice President Aaron Burr wrote his own epitaph:

AARON BURR
BORN FEB. 6TH 1756
DIED SEPT. 14TH 1836
A COLONEL IN THE ARMY OF THE
REVOLUTION
VICE PRESIDENT OF THE UNITED
STATES, FROM 1801 TO 1805.

*

Wife   Mother   Teacher
Pioneer   Woman
Crew Member, Space Shuttle Challenger
America's First Ordinary Citizen to Venture
Toward Space
She helped people. She laughed.
She loved and is loved.
She appreciated the world's natural beauty.
She was curious and sought to learn who we are and
what the universe is about. She relied on her own judgment
and moral courage to do right. She cared about the suffering
of her fellow man. She tried to protect our spaceship Earth.
She taught her children to do the same.
—Christa McAuliffe
EDUCATOR AND ASTRONAUT

He died in bed
–Doc Holliday
GUNFIGHTER

*

TRUTH AND HISTORY.
21 MEN.
THE BOY BANDIT KING
HE DIED AS HE LIVED
WILLIAM H. BONNEY
"BILLY THE KID"
–Billy the Kid
OUTLAW

*

Theologian and physician Albert Schweitzer once said
"In case my life should end with the cannibals,
I hope they will write on my tombstone":

WE HAVE EATEN DR. SCHWEITZER.

HE WAS GOOD TO THE END.

**WILLIAM CLARK
BORN IN VIRGINIA
AUGUST 1, 1770
ENTERED INTO LIFE ETERNAL
SEPTEMBER 1, 1838
SOLDIER, EXPLORER,
STATESMAN AND PATRIOT
HIS LIFE IS WRITTEN
IN THE HISTORY OF HIS COUNTRY.**
–William Clark
EXPLORER

*

On the Fourth of July, 1776,
He pledged his Life, Fortune and Sacred Honour
To the Independence of His Country.
On the third of September, 1783,
He affixed his Seal to the definitive Treaty with Great Britain
Which acknowledges that Independence,
And consummated the Redemption of his Pledge.
On the Fourth of July, 1826,
He was summoned
To the Independence of Immortality
And to the Judgment of his God.
–John Adams
U.S. PRESIDENT

Free at last, free at last
thank God almighty
I'm free at last.
—Martin Luther King Jr.
CIVIL RIGHTS ACTIVIST

✳

This cenotaph honors aviator Amelia Earhart:
Flew Atlantic Ocean solo
May 20–21, 1932
First to fly Pacific Ocean,
Honolulu to California, solo
January 11–12, 1935
Most famous and one of
the most beloved women fliers in history

✳

This inscription is on the wall behind U.S. President Ronald Reagan's grave:
I know in my heart that man is good
that what is right will always eventually triumph
and there is purpose and worth to each and every life.

The Gory Details

To
The Memory of
John Phillips
Accidentally Shot
as
A Mark of Affection by His
Brother.
–John Phillips

*

ALWAYS TIDY, NEAT AND CLEAN.
LOST HIS LIFE IN A SUBMARINE.
–Anonymous

*

On Thursday she was born,
On Thursday made a bride,
On Thursday her leg was broke,
And on Thursday she died.
–Anonymous

John Edwards died in a fire:
None could hold a candle to him.
–John Edwards

*

Here lie interred the dreadfully
bruised and lacerated bodies of
William Bradbury and Thomas his son
both of Greenfield who were together
savagely murdered in an unusually
horrid manner on a Monday Night, April 12 1832 . . .
Such interest did their tragic end excite
That, ere they were removed from human sight,
Thousands on thousands daily came to see
The bloody scene of the catastrophe . . .
–William and Thomas Bradbury

*

Here lies
Captain Ernest Bloomfield
Accidentally shot by his Orderly
March 2nd 1789
"Well done, thou good and faithful servant."
–Ernest Bloomfield

Underneath
this
Humble Stone
Sleeps a Skull
Of Name Unknown
Deep in Eden's Bed twas Found
As Ye Luckless Owner Drownd?
What Matter Since
We All Must Dye
Whether Death
Be Wet or Dry?
—Anonymous

*

IN MEMORY OF NODIAH BIRD
WHO WAS KILLED
BY AN INSANE PERSON MAY 17, 1835.
—Nodiah Bird

Sports Legends

Grace, Dignity and
Elegance Personified
–Joe DiMaggio
BASEBALL PLAYER

*

THE FATHER OF AMERICAN FOOTBALL
–Walter Camp
FOOTBALL COACH

*

A man's life is not important except
in the impact it has on other lives.
–Jackie Robinson
BASEBALL PLAYER

*

FOUNDER OF JEET KUNE DO
–Bruce Lee
MARTIAL ARTIST

Constantine D'Amato
A boy comes to me with a
spark of interest, I feed
the spark and it becomes
a flame, I feed the flame
and it becomes a fire, I
feed the fire and it becomes
a roaring blaze.
—CUS—
—Cus D'Amato
BOXING MANAGER AND TRAINER

＊

Cardinal Spellman wrote baseball player Babe Ruth's epitaph:
May the divine spirit that animated Babe Ruth to win the
crucial game of life inspire the youth of America.

＊

Distinguished Athlete, Scholar and Humanitarian
A Hard Road to Glory
—Arthur Ashe
TENNIS PLAYER

Heavyweight Champion of the World
1919–1926
A Gentle Man and a Gentleman
–Jack Dempsey
BOXER

*

Athlete Eric Liddell was portrayed in the film Chariots of Fire.
His epitaph reads:
They shall mount up with wings as eagles
They shall run, and not be weary.

*

There comes a time in every man's life
and I've had plenty of them.
–Casey Stengel
BASEBALL PLAYER

*

A magnificent New York Yankee,
true teammate and Hall of Fame centerfielder
with legendary courage.
The most popular player of his era.
A loving husband, father and friend for life.
–Mickey Mantle
BASEBALL PLAYER

Short and Silly Epitaphs

Oops! The stonecutter omitted the "e" in "Thine":
LORD, SHE IS THIN.
–Susannah Ensign

*

Here lies the body of Mary Ann Bent,
She kicked up her heels, and away she went.
–Mary Ann Bent

*

Leg of an Italian Sailor, 1898.
–Anonymous

*

Oh! Sun, Moon, Stars, and ye celestial Poles
Are graves then dwindled into button-holes?
–Button

*

She was in health at 11:30 A.M.
And left for Heaven at 3:30 P.M.
–Anonymous

Artists

Voice and Creator of Woody Woodpecker
–Gracie Lantz and Walter Lantz
ACTOR AND CARTOONIST

*

CHARLES M. SCHULZ SGT US ARMY WORLD WAR II
–Charles M. Schulz
CARTOONIST

*

Political cartoonist David Low suggested this epitaph for himself:

HERE LIES A NUISANCE DEDICATED TO SANITY.

What a Pity!

THE LEFT LEG & PART OF THE
THIGH OF HENRY HUGHES COOPER
WAS CUT OFF & INTERR'D HERE
JUNE 18TH 1759.
—Henry Hughes Cooper's Leg

*

A HOUSE SHE HATH, 'TIS MADE
OF SUCH GOOD FASHION,
THE TENANT NE'ER SHALL
PAY FOR REPARATION.
NOR WILL THE LANDLORD
EVER RAISE HER RENT
OR TURN HER OUT OF DOORS
FOR NONPAYMENT;
FROM CHIMNEY TAX THIS
CELL IS FREE.
TO SUCH A HOUSE WHO
WOULD NOT TENANT BE?
—Rebeca Bogess Folkestone

MY SHOES ARE MADE
MY WORK IS DONE
YES, DEAR FRIENDS, I'M GOING HOME
AND WHERE I'VE GONE
AND HOW I FARE
THERE'S NOBODY KNOWS
AND THERE'S NOBODY CARES.

–Francis Magranis

SHOEMAKER

*

Susanna Barford died at age 10:
This world to her was but a tragedy play,
she came and saw't, dislikt, and
pass'd away.

–Susanna Barford

Beloved Animals

BORN A DOG. DIED A GENTLEMAN.
—Major
DOG

*

Here lies
Copenhagen
the charger ridden by
the Duke of Wellington
the entire day, at the
Battle of Waterloo
Born 1808 Died 1836
God's humbler instrument though meaner clay,
should share the glory of that glorious day.
—Copenhagen
DUKE OF WELLINGTON'S HORSE

*

*Bonzo, the chimpanzee, co-starred with Ronald Reagan
in* Bedtime for Bonzo. *His epitaph reads:*
HE MADE US LAUGH

ROSA
MY FIRST JERSEY COW
RECORDED 2 LBS. 15 OZS. BUTTER
FROM 18 QTS. 1 DAY MILK.
—Rosa
COW

*

PRINT
?–1951
I HELPED DON
DELIVER HIS MAIL.
—Print
DOG

*

Here lies the body of my good horse,
The General. For twenty years he bore
me around the circuit of my practice,
and in all that time he never made a
blunder. Would that his master could say
the same!
—The General
U.S. PRESIDENT JOHN TYLER'S HORSE

In memory of
Maggie
Who in her time kicked
Two colonels,
Four majors,
Ten captains,
Twenty-four lieutenants,
Forty-two sergeants,
Four hundred and thirty-two other ranks
AND
One Mills Bomb.
–Maggie
ARMY MULE

*

TOPPER
HOPALONG CASSIDY'S
HORSE
–Topper
WILLIAM BOYD'S HORSE

Calculator
Born ?
Died Aug. 29, 1923
He made better dogs
of us all.
–Calculator
DOG AT INFANTRY SCHOOL IN GEORGIA

*

Here lies Bill. He done his damnedest.
–Bill
MULE

*

RASTAS
THE SMARTEST
MOST LOVEABLE
MONKEY
THAT EVER LIVED.
–Rastas
MONKEY

This epitaph for Boatswain, poet George Byron's beloved dog, may have been written by John Cam Hobhouse, Byron's close friend:

Near this Spot
are deposited the Remains of one
who possessed Beauty without Vanity,
Strength without Insolence,
Courage without Ferocity,
and all the Virtues of Man without his Vices.
This praise, which would be unmeaning Flattery,
if inscribed over human Ashes,
is but a just Tribute to the Memory of
BOATSWAIN, a *DOG*
who was born in *Newfoundland,* **May 1803,**
and died at *Newstead,* **Nov. 18, 1808.**

He Was a Good Guy

Here lies a man of good repute
Who wore a No. 16 Boot
'Tis not recorded how he died,
But sure it is that open wide
The gates of heaven must have been
To let such monstrous feet within.
—Anonymous

*

**SOON RIPE
SOON ROTTEN
SOON GONE
BUT NOT FORGOTTEN.**
—Milla Gaylord

*

AN UPRIGHT DOWNRIGHT HONEST MAN.
—John James

Jemima Jones
Passed on Jan 4 1803
This is the last long resting place
Of Aunt Jemima Jones
Her soul ascended into space
Amidst our tears and groans
She was not pleasing to the eye
Nor had she any brain
And when she talked twas through her nose
Which gave her friends much pain
But still we feel that she was worth
The money that was spent
Upon the coffin, hearse and stone
(The funeral plumes were lent).
–Jemima Jones

*

Here lies
JANE
SHORE
I say no more
Who was alive
in sixty-five
–Jane Shore

It is all right.
—**Charles Bowker**

*

Underneath this ancient pew
Lie the remains of Jonathan Blue;
His name was Black, but that wouldn't do.
—**Jonathan Black**

*

CHEERIO, SEE YOU SOON.
—**Anonymous**

*

IN JOYOUS MEMORY OF
GEORGE JONES
WHO WAS PRESIDENT OF
THE NEWPORT RIFLE CLUB
FOR TWENTY YEARS,
"ALWAYS MISSED."
—**George Jones**

Cautionary Tales

Mary, Sarah and Eliza Atwood . . . who were poisoned by eating
funguous vegetables mistaken for champignons
on the 11th day of October 1808 and died at the ages of 14, 7,
and 5 years within a few hours of each other in excruciating
circumstances. The Father, Mother and now, alas, an only child,
partakes of the same meal, have survived with debilitated
constitutions and to lament so dreadful a calumny. This monument
is erected to perpetuate the fatal events as an awful caution to
others, let it be too a solemn a warning that in our most grateful
enjoyments even in our necessary food may lurk deadly poison . . .
—Mary, Sarah, and Eliza Atwood

*

**DIED OF THIN SHOES, APRIL 17TH, 1839,
AGED 19 YEARS.**
—Julia Adams

*

Who killed Kildare?
Who dare Kildare to kill?
Death killed Kildare,
Who dare kill whom he will.
—Earl of Kildare

Underneath this sable Herse
Lies the Subject of all Verse:
Sydney's Sister, Pembroke's Mother—
Death! ere thou Kill'st such another
Fair, and good, and learnd as SHEE,
Time will throw his Dart at thee.
—Mary Herbert
COUNTESS OF PEMBROKE

*

*Barmaid Hannah Twynnoy was killed by a tiger who had escaped
from a circus. Her epitaph reads:*
In bloom of life
She's snatched from hence
She had not room
To make defence;
For Tiger fierce
Took life away,
And here she lies
In a bed of clay
Until the Resurrection Day.

*

This is the grave of Mike O'Day
Who died maintaining his right of way.
His right was clear, his will was strong.
But he's just as dead as if he'd been wrong.
—Mike O'Day

The chief concern of her life for the last
twenty-five years was to order and provide
for her funeral. Her greatest pleasure
was to think and talk about it. She lived
many years on a pension of 9d per week,
and yet she saved £5, which at her own
request was laid out on her funeral.
—Mary Broomfield

*

Here lies THOMAS HUDDLESTONE. Reader, don't smile!
But reflect as this tombstone you view,
That death, who kill'd him, in a very short while
Will *huddle* a *stone* upon you.
—Thomas Huddlestone

*

**STOP STRANGER AS YOU PASS BY
AS YOU ARE NOW SO ONCE WAS I
AS I AM NOW SO WILL YOU BE
SO BE PREPARED TO FOLLOW ME.**
—Anonymous

𝔚riters

I'm A Writer
but then
Nobody's Perfect
–Billy Wilder
WRITER

*

Novelist-Citizen of two countries—Interpreter of his
generation on both sides of the sea.
–Henry James
WRITER

*

OVER MY DEAD BODY.
–George S. Kaufman
WRITER

*

*This quotation is from poet W. H. Auden's elegy on fellow poet
William Butler Yeats:*
In the prison of his days
teach the free man how to praise.

A Merry Heart
–Upton Sinclair
WRITER

*

HOMO SUM! THE ADVENTURER.
–D. H. Lawrence
WRITER

*

Writer William S. Burroughs planned his own epitaph:
Father Breath once more farewell,
Birth you gave was no thing ill,
My heart is still as time will tell.

*

THE FIRST AND GREATEST OF WAR CORRESPONDENTS.
–William Howard Russell
WRITER

*

Writer Robert Benchley suggested this epitaph for himself:
ALL OF THIS IS OVER MY HEAD.

Writer Ben Travers suggested this epitaph for himself:

THIS IS WHERE THE REAL FUN STARTS.

*

Writer Thomas Hardy wanted to be buried in Dorset. After he passed away, the Literary Executor and supervisor of Poet's Corner at Westminster Abbey insisted that Hardy be buried in the Abbey. Eventually a compromise was made: Hardy's heart was buried in Dorset and his ashes were placed in Westminster Abbey. His heart now lies in the same grave as his first and second wives. His epitaph reads:

HERE LIES THE HEART OF THOMAS HARDY O.M. SON OF THOMAS AND JEMIMA HARDY.

–Thomas Hardy

WRITER

*

Writer H. G. Wells suggested this epitaph for himself:

I TOLD YOU SO, DAMMIT!

–H. G. Wells

WRITER

In Memory of
JANE AUSTEN
youngest daughter of the late
Revd GEORGE AUSTEN,
formerly Rector of Steventon in this County,
She departed this Life on the 18th of July, 1817,
aged 41, after a long illness supported with
the patience and the hopes of a Christian.
The benevolence of her heart,
the sweetness of her temper, and
the extraordinary endowments of her mind
obtained the regard of all who knew her, and
the warmest love of her intimate connections.
Their grief is in proportion to their affection,
they know their loss to be irreparable,
but in their deepest affliction they are consoled
by a firm though humble hope that her charity,
devotion, faith and purity, rendered
her soul acceptable in the sight of her
REDEEMER.
–Jane Austen
WRITER

Writer Erma Bombeck suggested this epitaph for herself:

BIG DEAL! I'M USED TO DUST.
–Erma Bombeck
WRITER

*

BE MY EPITAPH WRIT ON MY COUNTRY'S MIND, "HE SERVED HIS COUNTRY AND LOVED HIS KIND."
–Thomas Davis
WRITER

*

News broadcaster Huw Wheldon suggested this epitaph for himself:
He never used a sentence
where a paragraph would do.

*

Writer Ernest Hemingway suggested this epitaph for himself:

PARDON ME FOR NOT GETTING UP.

This inscription is on a monument honoring writer Thomas Paine:
"The world is my country;
To do good my religion."
Thomas Paine
Author of
Common Sense
Born in England, January 29, 1737
Died in New York City, June 8, 1809
"The palaces of kings are built upon
the ruins of the bowers of Paradise."
—Common Sense

*

In Loving Memory of
My Brother
Clive Staples Lewis
Born Belfast 29th November 1898
Died in this parish
22nd November 1963
Men must endure their going hence.
—C. S. Lewis
WRITER

A TALENT TO AMUSE.
–Noël Coward
WRITER

✳

Writer Dorothy Parker suggested this epitaph for herself:
IF YOU CAN READ THIS YOU ARE STANDING TOO CLOSE.

✳

Good friend, for Jesu's sake forbeare
To dig the dust enclosed here;
Blessed be he that spares these stones,
And curst be he that moves my bones.
–William Shakespeare
WRITER

✳

Called back.
–Emily Dickinson
POET

Musings:
Poking Fun at Death

Throughout the ages, mortals have made fun of death. In the grand scheme of things, humor doesn't change death, but it certainly numbs a little of its sting. This chapter is loaded with a full arsenal of sarcastic and cynical remarks about Death and his friends, the cemetery, the funeral, and the obituary notice.

There is plenty to laugh about here, like the absurdity of putting a fence around a cemetery and the spectacle of some high-profile funerals. You'll also get advice on the worst kind of book to be caught with on your bedside table if you end up dying in the middle of the night. It's important to think of such things because Death could come knocking at any time. And of course, there are plenty of jokes about death and taxes, undertakers, and epitaphs that fudge the truth.

These quotations are irreverent, flippant, and extremely blunt. The humor lies in the brutal honesty and slightly bitter tone. It's like eating a whole bag of sweet and sour gummy worms. They're delightfully sour, and you can't stop at one.

Comedians like Robin Williams, George Burns, and Woody Allen take jabs at Death. Literary wits like Mark Twain, Noël Coward, and Oscar Wilde wipe the floor with Death. They take no prisoners. It's okay to snicker, chuckle, and even laugh out loud. The dead won't mind.

The Unwelcome Visitor

Death comes along like a gas bill one can't pay—
and that's all one can say about it.
—Anthony Burgess
WRITER

♣

Death is hacking away at my address book and party lists.
—Mason Cooley
WRITER

♣

DEATH IS NATURE'S WAY OF SAYING,
"YOUR TABLE IS READY."
—Robin Williams
ACTOR

♣

If you are small, death may quite likely overlook you.
—W. Somerset Maugham
WRITER

Actor Edith Evans made this comment one week before her death:
Death is my neighbor now.

✤

Poet Horace Smith described death as:
THE SLEEPING PARTNER OF LIFE.

✤

I want death to find me planting
my cabbages, but caring little for it,
and much more for my imperfect garden.
–Michel de Montaigne
WRITER

✤

DEATH RIDES A FAST CAMEL.
–Arabic proverb

✤

Everything comes to him who waits—among other things, death.
–Francis Herbert Bradley
PHILOSOPHER

✤

Death sneaks up on you like a windshield sneaks up on a bug.
–Anonymous

Dying Properly

People are always dying in the *New York Times* who
don't seem to die in other papers, and they die at a
greater length and maybe even with a little more grace.
–James Reston
WRITER

❖

Dying ought to be done in black and white.
It is simply not a colorful activity.
–Russell Baker
WRITER

❖

**IF THIS IS DYING,
I DON'T THINK MUCH OF IT.**
–Lytton Strachey
WRITER

❖

It is but a few short years from diapers to dignity
and from dignity to decomposition!
–Don Herold
WRITER

I was sorry to have my name mentioned as one of the
great authors, because they have a sad habit of dying off.
Chaucer is dead, Spenser is dead, so is Milton,
so is Shakespeare, and I am not feeling very well myself.
–Mark Twain
WRITER

✤

I'm trying to die correctly, but it's very difficult, you know.
–Lawrence Durrell
WRITER

✤

WHY DO DYING PEOPLE NEVER SHED TEARS?
–Max Frisch
WRITER

✤

Writer S. N. Behrman commented on being 75 years old:
I HAVE HAD JUST ABOUT ALL I CAN TAKE OF MYSELF.

There is a sense in which the dying *shake off* the concerns
of the living, play them like a salmon plays the rod—
seeming to get a little better so that relief replaces concern,
then worsening again so that anxiety returns. It needs only a
short dose of this before the living are quite glad to see them go.
—Alan Bennett
WRITER

❖

**TO HELL WITH REALITY!
I WANT TO DIE IN MUSIC,
NOT IN REASON OR IN PROSE.**
—Louis-Ferdinand Céline
WRITER

❖

True you can't take it with you, but then that's not the place
where it comes in handy.
—Brendan Francis Behan
WRITER

When writer Katherine Ann Porter was 80 years old,
she made this comment about death:
I'm not afraid of life and I'm not afraid of death:
Dying's the bore.

♣

I AM DYING WITH THE HELP
OF TOO MANY PHYSICIANS.
−Alexander the Great
KING OF MACEDON

♣

WHEN GOOD AMERICANS DIE,
THEY GO TO PARIS;
WHEN BAD AMERICANS DIE,
THEY GO TO AMERICA.
−Oscar Wilde
WRITER

Corpses, Coffins, and Undertakers, Oh My!

As dead as a doornail.
—Proverb

♣

DEAD MEN BITE NOT.
—Latin proverb

♣

Shrouds have no pockets.
—Folk saying

♣

Writer Elbert Hubbard described the coffin as:
A ROOM WITHOUT A DOOR OR A SKYLIGHT.

♣

Coffins have also been dubbed:
A container small enough for bums, large enough for presidents.
—Anonymous

Politician Claiborne Pell commented on life in Washington, D.C.:
People only leave by way of the box—ballot or coffin.

♣

Alas, poor Yorick! How surprised he would be
to see how his counterpart
of today is whisked off to a funeral parlor
and is in short order sprayed,
sliced, pierced, pickled, trussed, trimmed, creamed, waxed,
painted, rouged and neatly dressed—transformed from
a common corpse into a Beautiful Memory Picture.
–Jessica Mitford
WRITER

♣

**THE OLD NEIGHBORHOOD HAS CHANGED.
HURLEY BROTHERS FUNERAL HOME
IS NOW CALLED DEATH 'N' THINGS.
–Elmore Leonard**
WRITER

An undertaker does not have much use for a living man
but he has great respect for a dead one.
–Charles A. Boutelle
POLITICIAN

✤

MY UNCLE IS A SOUTHERN PLANTER.
HE'S AN UNDERTAKER IN ALABAMA.
–Fred Allen
ACTOR

✤

Dust to dust, ashes to ashes, and the cremains to a memorial park.
All this is supposed to maintain the dignity of death.
Or is it the dignity of undertakers?
–Joseph Wood Krutch
WRITER

Funeral Mayhem

A damn good funeral is still one of our best
and cheapest acts of theatre.
—Gwyn Thomas
WRITER

❖

*Actor Red Skelton remarked about the huge attendance at
movie mogul Harry Cohn's funeral:*
Well, it only proves what they always say—give the
public something they want to see, and they'll come out for it!

❖

No matter how rich you become, how famous or powerful,
when you die the size of your funeral will still pretty
much depend on the weather.
—Michael Pritchard
MOTIVATIONAL SPEAKER

❖

Manager and trainer Jack Hurley said these words about boxer Vince Foster:
At his funeral in Omaha he filled the church to capacity.
He was a draw right to the finish.

Writer Mark Twain decided not to go to the funeral
of a corrupt politician:

I REFUSED TO ATTEND HIS FUNERAL, BUT I WROTE A VERY NICE LETTER EXPLAINING THAT I APPROVED OF IT.

✤

Writer Arthur Miller was asked if he would attend the funeral of his
ex-wife Marilyn Monroe:

WHY SHOULD I GO? SHE WON'T BE THERE.

✤

Writer George Bernard Shaw decided not to go to Washington Irving's funeral:
Literature, alas, has no place in his death as it had no place in his life. Irving would turn in his coffin if I came, just as Shakespeare will turn in his coffin when Irving comes.

✤

IN THE CITY A FUNERAL IS JUST AN INTERRUPTION OF TRAFFIC. IN THE COUNTRY IT IS A FORM OF POPULAR ENTERTAINMENT.
–George Ade
WRITER

I had a friend who was a clown. When he died, all his friends went to the funeral in one car.
–Steven Wright
COMEDIAN

♣

The driver of a hearse has the advantage of never having to put up with backseat driving.
–Douglas Yates

♣

[MEMORIAL SERVICES ARE THE] COCKTAIL PARTIES OF THE GERIATRIC SET.
–Ralph Richardson
ACTOR

♣

Writer Leonard L. Levinson described the funeral as:
THE LAST BEDTIME STORY.

♣

[F]unerals are always occasions for pious lying. A deep vein of superstition and a sudden touch of kindness always lead people to give the departed credit for more virtues than he possessed.
–I. F. Stone
WRITER

The last [funeral] I went to had people in the front pew that I
wouldn't have to my funeral over my dead body.

—Anonymous

❖

By the time an actor gets ready to die he hasn't enough friends left
out there to act as pallbearers. At most funerals the six men you
see motivating the casket are from Central Casting.

—Fred Allen

ACTOR

❖

Actor Clark Gable wanted his funeral to be held closed-casket:

**I DON'T WANT A LOT OF STRANGERS
LOOKING DOWN AT MY WRINKLES
AND MY BIG FAT BELLY WHEN I'M DEAD.**

❖

There is to be a public lying-in-state for Gertie [Lawrence],
in which she will wear the pink dress in which she danced the
polka in *The King and I.* Vulgarity can go no further.

—Noël Coward

WRITER

*Writer Hans Christian Andersen gave particular instructions
for the music for his funeral:*
Most of the people who will walk after me will be children,
so make the beat keep time with short steps.

✛

Writer P. J. O'Rourke described modern-day funerals:
As anyone familiar with modern fiction
and motion pictures knows, excessive grief cannot be expressed by
means of tears or a mournful face. It is necessary to break things,
hit people, and throw yourself onto the top
of the coffin, at least.

✛

Anything awful makes me laugh. I misbehaved once at a funeral.
–Charles Lamb
WRITER

✛

There is nothing like a morning funeral for
sharpening the appetite for lunch.
–Arthur Marshall
WRITER

Someone once described death as:
When man is put to bed with a shovel.
—Anonymous

♣

THE GUY WHO INVENTED THE HOKEY-POKEY JUST DIED. IT WAS A WEIRD FUNERAL. FIRST, THEY PUT HIS LEFT LEG IN . . .
—Irv Gilman
COMEDIAN

♣

ALL I DESIRE FOR MY OWN BURIAL IS NOT TO BE BURIED ALIVE.
—Philip Dormer Stanhope
POLITICIAN

♣

They say such nice things about people at their funerals that it makes me sad to realize I'm going to miss mine by just a few days.
—Garrison Keillor
WRITER

Belated Praise

I read the *Times* and if my name is not in the obits
I proceed to enjoy the day.
–Noël Coward
WRITER

♣

I have never wanted to see anybody die, but there are a
few obituary notices I have read with pleasure.
–Clarence Darrow
LAWYER

♣

By request of showman P. T. Barnum, the New York Evening Sun *published
his obituary in advance so that he could read it. Here is the headline
from his obituary published on March 24, 1891 (two weeks before his death):*

GREAT AND ONLY BARNUM.
HE WANTED TO READ HIS OBITUARY;
HERE IT IS.

The only thing that really saddens me over my demise
is that I shall not be here to read the nonsense that will be written
about me . . . There will be lists of apocryphal jokes I never made
and gleeful misquotations of words I never said.
What a pity I shan't be here to enjoy them!
−Noël Coward
WRITER

✣

**Epitaph: a belated advertisement
for a line that
has been permanently discontinued.**
−Irvin S. Cobb
WRITER

✣

The rarest quality in an epitaph is truth.
−Henry David Thoreau
WRITER

✣

He is a good man—according to his epitaph.
−Jewish saying

The tombstone is about the only thing that can stand upright and lie on its face at the same time.
–Mary Wilson Little
WRITER

✤

Writer Elbert Hubbard described the epitaph as:

POSTPONED COMPLIMENTS.

✤

Satire does not look pretty on a tombstone.
–Charles Lamb
WRITER

The Ultimate Hangout

Grave, *n*. A place in which the dead are laid to await
the coming of the medical student.
—Ambrose Bierce
WRITER

♣

An odd thought strikes me—
we shall receive no letters in the grave.
—Samuel Johnson
POET

♣

THE GRAVE IS THE GENERAL MEETING PLACE.
—Proverb

♣

Writer Washington Irving described the grave as:
[A place that] busies every error—covers every defect—
extinguishes every resentment!

**A GRAVE IS BUT A PLAIN SUIT, AND A RICH
MONUMENT IS ONE EMBROIDERED.**
–Thomas Fuller
CLERGYMAN

❖

Someone once described the monument as:
A boast in stone.
–Anonymous

❖

The monuments of the nations are all protests against nothingness
after death; so are statues and inscriptions; so is history.
–Lew Wallace
UNION ARMY GENERAL DURING THE AMERICAN CIVIL WAR

❖

After I'm dead I'd rather have people ask why
I have no monument than why I have one.
–Cato the Elder
POLITICIAN

The fence around a cemetery is foolish, for those inside can't come out and those outside don't want to get in.
–Arthur Brisbane
WRITER

✤

Someone once described the cemetery as:
The place which receives all without asking questions.
–Anonymous

✤

PROMOTION COMETH NEITHER FROM
EAST NOR WEST,
BUT FROM THE CEMETERY.
–Edward Sanford Martin
WRITER

✤

The cemetery was called this by Eugene E. Brussell:
MAN'S FINAL COMMENT ON EARTH.

CEMETERY, N. AN ISOLATED SUBURBAN SPOT WHERE MOURNERS MATCH LIES, POETS WRITE AT A TARGET AND STONECUTTERS SPELL FOR A WAGER.

–Ambrose Bierce

WRITER

♣

The graveyards are full of indispensable men.

–Charles de Gaulle

PRESIDENT OF THE FRENCH REPUBLIC

♣

Writer Mark Twain called the cemetery:

THE COUNTRY HOME I NEED.

Better Off

It's funny the way most people love the dead.
Once you are dead, you are made for life.
–Jimi Hendrix
MUSICIAN

❖

Nowadays the real danger to dead authors isn't the
malicious biography but the avaricious sequel.
–David Grylls
EDUCATOR

❖

I'll welcome death—no more interviews!
–Katharine Hepburn
ACTOR

❖

When a man dies, and his kin are glad of it, they say,
"He is better off."
–Edgar Watson Howe
WRITER

For three days after death, hair and fingernails
continue to grow, but phone calls taper off.
–Johnny Carson
ACTOR

❧

Since we have to speak well
of the dead, let's knock them while they're alive.
–John Sloan
ARTIST

❧

When writer Dorothy Parker was 70 years old,
she made this comment about death:
IF I HAD ANY DECENCY, I'D BE DEAD.
MOST OF MY FRIENDS ARE.

❧

U.S. Postmaster General James Edward Day received a letter
from someone who wanted their portrait on a postage stamp.
He wrote this note but didn't mail it:
We cannot put the face of a person on a stamp unless said person
is deceased. My suggestion, therefore is that you drop dead.

The poor wish to be rich, the rich wish to be happy, the single wish to be married, and the married wish to be dead.
–Ann Landers
WRITER

❖

THE LIVING ARE THE DEAD ON HOLIDAY.
–Maurice Maeterlinck
WRITER

❖

Actor Jimmy Durante once explained why he gave money to panhandlers:
Maybe we ain't born equal, but it's a cinch we all die equal.

❖

Death ends a life, not a relationship.
–Jack Lemmon
ACTOR

❖

I NEVER THINK THAT PEOPLE DIE.
THEY JUST GO TO DEPARTMENT STORES.
–Andy Warhol
ARTIST

DEATH, THE CLICHÉ ASSURES US,
IS THE GREAT LEVELER; BUT IT
OBVIOUSLY LEVELS SOME A GREAT
DEAL MORE THAN OTHERS.

—Alden Whitman

WRITER

✥

No matter who you are, you only get a little slice of the world.
Have you ever seen a hearse followed by a U-Haul?

—Billy Graham

CHRISTIAN EVANGELIST

✥

I don't think anything is ever quite
the same to us after we are dead.

—Don Marquis

WRITER

✥

Every man of genius is considerably helped by being dead.

—Robert Lynd

WRITER

Death and Money

In this world nothing can be said to be certain,
except death and taxes.
—Benjamin Franklin
POLITICAL LEADER OF THE AMERICAN REVOLUTION

✢

I've got all the money I'll ever need if I die by four o'clock.
—Henry Youngman
COMEDIAN

✢

If the rich could hire other people to die for them,
the poor could make a wonderful living.
—Yiddish proverb

✢

It costs a lot of money to die comfortably.
—Samuel Butler
WRITER

✢

The difference between death and taxes
is that death never gets any worse.
—Anonymous

The Recently Departed

ANY AMUSING DEATHS LATELY?
—Maurice Bowra
SCHOLAR

✣

Writer Mark Twain's cousin, James Ross Clemens, was ill in London. Newspapers confused the two of them and reported that Mark Twain was either ill or dead in London. Twain set the truth straight with this famous remark:

THE REPORT OF MY DEATH WAS AN EXAGGERATION.

✣

Someone once sent this witty telegram:

REGRET TO INFORM YOU HAND THAT ROCKED THE CRADLE KICKED THE BUCKET.
—Anonymous

✣

Writer Gore Vidal made the following remark after Truman Capote died:

GOOD CAREER MOVE.

WHAT EINSTEIN WAS TO PHYSICS, WHAT BABE RUTH WAS TO HOME RUNS, WHAT EMILY POST WAS TO TABLE MANNERS . . . THAT'S WHAT EDWARD G. ROBINSON WAS TO DYING LIKE A DIRTY RAT.

–Russell Baker

WRITER

❖

*Broadway producer Charles B. Dillingham commented on
Harry Houdini's coffin:*

I BET YOU A HUNDRED BUCKS HE AIN'T IN HERE.

❖

Death seems to provide the minds of the Anglo-Saxon race
with a greater fund of innocent amusement than any other
single subject . . . the tale must be about dead bodies or very
wicked people, preferably both, before the Tired Business
Man can feel really happy.

–Dorothy L. Sayers

WRITER

While other people's deaths are deeply sad,
one's own is surely a bit of a joke.
–James Cameron
FILM DIRECTOR

✣

Writer Dorothy Parker said the following words after
Calvin Coolidge passed away:
HOW DO THEY KNOW?

✣

Jimmy Hoffa's most valuable contribution
to the American labour movement came at the moment
he stopped breathing—on July 30th, 1975.
–Don E. Moldea
WRITER

✣

WHEN I DIE, THE WORLD WILL HEAVE A GREAT SIGH OF RELIEF.
–Napoleon I
EMPEROR OF FRANCE AND KING OF ITALY

We met . . . Dr. Hall in such very deep mourning that either his mother, his wife, or himself must be dead.

–Jane Austen

WRITER

♣

Singer Janis Joplin's photograph was supposed to appear on the cover of Newsweek, *but it was replaced with a photograph of U.S. President Eisenhower after his death. She responded:*

FOURTEEN HEART ATTACKS AND HE HAD TO DIE IN MY WEEK.

♣

Writer William Connor, also known by his pen name Cassandra, wrote about Joseph Stalin's death:

FEW MEN BY THEIR DEATH CAN HAVE GIVEN SUCH DEEP SATISFACTION TO SO MANY.

A Full Life

I don't want to get to the end of my life and find that I just
lived the length of it. I want to have lived the width of it as well.
–Diane Ackerman
WRITER

❖

If you bemoan your brief stay on earth, consider the mayfly
which lives only for one day. If the weather were bad that day,
your whole life could be rained out.
–Wes "Scoop" Nisker
WRITER

❖

I do really think that death will be marvellous . . .
If there wasn't death, I think you couldn't go on.
–Stevie Smith
POET

❖

Life is a great big canvas; throw all the paint you can at it.
–Danny Kaye
ACTOR

**OUR DEATH IS NOT AN END IF WE
CAN LIVE ON IN OUR CHILDREN
AND THE YOUNGER GENERATION.
FOR THEY ARE US; OUR BODIES ARE ONLY
WILTED LEAVES ON THE TREE OF LIFE.**
–Albert Einstein
PHYSICIST

✣

If you're going to die, die doing what you love to do.
–Bernard Shaw
WRITER

✣

While others may argue about whether the world ends
with a bang or a whimper, I just want to make sure mine
doesn't end with a whine.
–Barbara Gordon
TELEVISION PRODUCER

✣

**IF I COULD DROP DEAD RIGHT NOW,
I'D BE THE HAPPIEST MAN ALIVE!**
–Samuel Goldwyn
FILM PRODUCER

Many people's tombstones should read,
"Died at 30. Buried at 60."
—Nicholas Murray Butler
EDUCATOR

♣

I POSTPONE DEATH BY LIVING,
BY SUFFERING, BY ERROR,
BY RISKING, BY GIVING, BY LOVING.
—Anaïs Nin
WRITER

♣

Whenever I prepare for a journey I prepare as for death. Should I
never return, all is in order. This is what life has taught me.
—Katherine Mansfield
WRITER

♣

If my doctor told me I only had six minutes to live,
I wouldn't brood. I'd type a little faster.
—Isaac Asimov
WRITER

**AS A WELL-SPENT DAY
BRINGS HAPPY SLEEP,
SO LIFE WELL USED
BRINGS HAPPY DEATH.**
–Leonardo da Vinci
ARTIST

✤

Of all the deathbed regrets that I have heard not one
of them has been, "I wish I had spent more time at the office."
–Wayne Dyer
MOTIVATIONAL SPEAKER

✤

Dying seems less sad than having lived too little.
–Gloria Steinem
WRITER

✤

I look back on my life like a good day's work,
it was done and I am satisfied with it.
–Grandma Moses
ARTIST

Beyond the Horizon

We have always held to the hope, the belief, the conviction that there is a better life, a better world, beyond the horizon.
–Franklin D. Roosevelt
U.S. PRESIDENT

❧

Writer Helen Keller explained death with the following words:
Death . . . is no more than passing from one room into another. But there's a difference for me, you know. Because in that other room I shall be able to see.

❧

DEATH IS ONLY A LARGER KIND OF GOING ABROAD.
–Samuel Butler
WRITER

❧

My idea of heaven is eating *pâté de foie gras* to the sound of trumpets.
–Sydney Smith
WRITER

DEATH IS BUT CROSSING THE WORLD, AS FRIENDS DO THE SEAS; THEY LIVE IN ONE ANOTHER STILL.

–William Penn

FOUNDER OF THE PROVINCE OF PENNSYLVANIA

❖

Death is simply a shedding of the physical body,
like the butterfly coming out of a cocoon . . . It's like putting away
your winter coat when spring comes.

–Elisabeth Kübler-Ross

PSYCHIATRIST

❖

HEAVEN IS A PLACE WHERE YOU GET AN OPPORTUNITY TO USE ALL THE MILLIONS OF SENSITIVITIES YOU NEVER KNEW YOU HAD BEFORE.

–Duke Ellington

COMPOSER

❖

When one man dies, one chapter is not torn out of the book,
but translated into a better language.

–John Donne

WRITER

The Honest Truth about Death

Death is just around the corner. If only it would stay there.
—Mason Cooley
WRITER

♣

YOU HAVEN'T LIVED UNTIL
YOU'VE DIED IN CALIFORNIA.
—Mort Sahl
ACTOR

♣

Of all escape mechanisms, death is the most efficient.
—H. L. Mencken
WRITER

♣

Death is nature's way of saying "Howdy."
—Anonymous

♣

I still go up my forty-four stairs two at a time, but that is in hopes
of dropping dead at the top.
—A. E. Houseman
POET

When you don't have any money, the problem is food.
When you have money, it's sex. When you have both, it's health.
If everything is simply jake, then you're frightened of death.
–J. P. Donleavy
WRITER

❖

ON THE PLUS SIDE, DEATH
IS ONE OF THE FEW THINGS
THAT CAN BE DONE AS EASILY
LYING DOWN.
–Woody Allen
FILM DIRECTOR AND WRITER

❖

**DEATH IS JUST A DISTANT RUMOR
TO THE YOUNG.**
–Andy Rooney
WRITER

❖

The good old horse-and-buggy days: then you lived until you died
and not until you were just run over.
–Will Rogers
ACTOR

DEATH IS THE GREATEST KICK OF ALL, THAT'S WHY THEY SAVE IT FOR LAST.
–Robert Reisner
WRITER

✤

The trouble with heart disease is that the first symptom
is often hard to deal with: sudden death.
–Michael Phelps
PHYSICIAN

✤

The riders in a race do not stop when they reach the goal.
There is a little finishing canter before coming to a standstill.
There is time to hear the kind voices of friends and say to oneself,
"The work is done."
–Oliver Wendell Holmes Sr.
POET

✤

Depend upon it, Sir, when a man knows he is to be hanged in a
fortnight, it concentrates his mind wonderfully.
–Samuel Johnson
POET

**THE BEST OF US BEING UNFIT TO DIE,
WHAT AN INEXPRESSIBLE
ABSURDITY TO PUT THE WORST TO DEATH!**
–Nathaniel Hawthorne
WRITER

✤

When we die, it's sure enough for the first time. I'll be interested
to see how it comes out, but I'm in no hurry.
–Ray Charles
SINGER

✤

There is no reason for me to die. I already died in Altoona.
–George Burns
ACTOR

✤

**I HOPE THE EXIT IS JOYFUL–AND
I HOPE NEVER TO COME BACK.**
–Frida Kahlo
ARTIST

✤

When I die, I'm going to leave my body to science fiction.
–Steven Wright
COMEDIAN

Only death goes deeper than sex.
–Mason Cooley
WRITER

♣

Exercise daily. Eat wisely. Die anyway.
–Anonymous

♣

I often wonder how I'm going to die.
You don't want to embarrass friends.
–Cary Grant
ACTOR

♣

DEATH IS NATURE'S WAY OF
TELLING YOU TO SLOW DOWN.
–Severn Darden
ACTOR

♣

Although prepared for martyrdom,
I preferred that it be postponed.
–Winston Churchill
PRIME MINISTER OF THE UNITED KINGDOM

If you die in the elevator, be sure to push the UP button.
–Sam Levenson
WRITER

❖

**DYING IS THE MOST EMBARRASSING THING
THAT CAN EVER HAPPEN TO YOU,
BECAUSE SOMEONE'S GOT TO
TAKE CARE OF ALL YOUR DETAILS.**
–Andy Warhol
ARTIST

❖

Life is a punctuated paragraph—diseases are the commas, sickness
the semicolons, and death the full stop.
–Josh Billings
WRITER

❖

IT'S NOT THAT I'M AFRAID TO DIE.
I JUST DON'T WANT TO BE THERE
WHEN IT HAPPENS.
–Woody Allen
FILM DIRECTOR AND WRITER

I cannot forgive my friends for dying; I do not find
these vanishing acts of theirs at all amusing.
–Logan Pearsall Smith
WRITER

❖

Even very young children need to be informed about dying.
Explain the concept of death very carefully to your child. This will
make threatening him with it much more effective.
–P. J. O'Rourke
WRITER

❖

**IF MR. SELWYN CALLS AGAIN,
SHOW HIM UP: IF I AM ALIVE
I SHALL BE DELIGHTED TO SEE HIM;
AND IF I AM DEAD
HE WOULD LIKE TO SEE ME.**
–Henry Fox
POLITICIAN

❖

I've been doing nothing but writing royal letters of condolence. I
said to Benita [Hume] on the telephone that all I expected from
my friends nowadays was that they should live through dinner.
–Noël Coward
WRITER

I DON'T BELIEVE IN DYING. IT'S BEEN DONE. I'M WORKING ON A NEW EXIT. BESIDES, I CAN'T DIE NOW– I'M BOOKED.

–George Burns

ACTOR

✤

DON'T READ SCIENCE FICTION BOOKS. IT'LL LOOK BAD IF YOU DIE IN BED WITH ONE ON THE NIGHTSTAND. ALWAYS READ STUFF THAT WILL MAKE YOU LOOK GOOD IF YOU DIE IN THE MIDDLE OF THE NIGHT.

–P. J. O'Rourke

WRITER

✤

The trouble with quotes about death is that 99.999 percent of them are made by people who are still alive.

–Joshua Bruns

WRITER

Farewells:
Last Words to Die By

ALL OF THE PEOPLE in the pages ahead made their "grand exit" memorable. Some died of illness, and others died in battle. Some deaths were anticipated, while others were unexpected. No matter how each person exits, it is *their* moment, their glorious and unique final scene.

Many of the speakers in this chapter were suffering from illness. Their schedules consisted of visits from physicians, friends, and family. There was also plenty of time for contemplating their lives and appreciating the view from their rooms. Their last words reflect their busy days, whether they were trying to finish up work or settle on their burial arrangements.

There are also several quotations uttered before unexpected deaths, such as suicides and assassinations. These words are especially poignant because they were merely ordinary statements. Some of the last words from battle have a poetic touch, such as Robert E. Lee's words, "Strike the tent."

Many of these famous figures were content in their last moments. They were satisfied with how they had lived their lives. They advised their friends on how to carry on their legacies. Some of them looked forward to the next adventure.

Each quotation is beautiful in its own way. Each one reflects courage and humanity. May this collection of last words entertain and inspire contemplation—and a few chuckles.

I'm Ready to Go

I have done all that I was sent into the world to do,
and I am ready to go.
–C. S. Lewis
WRITER

✠

How you die is the most important thing you
ever do. It's the exit, the final scene of the glorious
epic of your life. It's the third act and, you know, everything
builds up to the third act.
–Timothy Leary
PSYCHOLOGIST

✠

OH! THIS IS THE LAST OF ALL.
–Franz Schubert
COMPOSER

✠

I MUST GO IN, THE FOG IS RISING.
–Emily Dickinson
POET

I am about to die, I expect the summons soon.
I have endeavored to discharge all my official duties faithfully.
I regret nothing, but am sorry that I am about to leave my friends.
—Zachary Taylor
U.S. PRESIDENT

⚜

I GO TO SEE THE SUN FOR THE LAST TIME.
—Jean-Jacques Rousseau
PHILOSOPHER

⚜

My friend, the artery ceases to beat.
—Albrecht von Haller
ANATOMIST

⚜

DRAW THE CURTAIN:
THE FARCE IS ENDED.
—François Rabelais
WRITER

⚜

I am going. Perhaps it is for the best.
—John Tyler
U.S. PRESIDENT

Now all is over. Let the piper play "Return No More."
—Rob Roy
OUTLAW

✛

I am a broken machine. I am ready to go.
—Woodrow Wilson
U.S. PRESIDENT

✛

Banker Jay Cooke listened to the prayer for the dying:
THAT WAS THE RIGHT PRAYER.

✛

I believe . . . I'm going to die. I love the rain.
I want the feeling of it on my face.
—Katherine Mansfield
WRITER

✛

My name and memory I leave to man's charitable speeches,
to foreign nations and to the next age.
—Francis Bacon
PHILOSOPHER

Send in the Visitors

Actor Ingrid Bergman freshened up for a visitor:
Do I look all right? Give me my brush and makeup.

❖

In his final days, poet Samuel Johnson suffered from fits of delirium:
What, will that fellow never have done talking poetry to me?

❖

HOW IMPERIOUS ONE IS
WHEN ONE NO LONGER HAS
THE TIME TO BE POLITE.
–Jeanne-Louise-Henriette Campan
EDUCATOR

❖

That's good. Go on. Read some more.
–Warren G. Harding
U.S. PRESIDENT

❖

Refresh me with a great thought.
–Johann Gottfried von Herder
POET

Taking Care of Business

HOW WERE THE CIRCUS RECEIPTS TONIGHT AT MADISON SQUARE GARDEN?
–P. T. Barnum

SHOWMAN

❖

Composer Eugène Ysaÿe listened to his Fourth Sonata:
Splendid . . . the finale just a little too fast.

❖

TEXAS RECOGNIZED. ARCHER TOLD ME SO. DID YOU SEE IT IN THE PAPERS?
–Stephen F. Austin

"THE FATHER OF TEXAS"

❖

Writer Honoré de Balzac penned the following:
I can no longer read or write.

Monks! Monks! Monks!
–Henry VIII
KING OF ENGLAND

❖

Actor Gertrude Lawrence's last words were about her Broadway co-star,
Yul Brynner, in The King and I:
See that Yul [Brynner] gets star billing. He has earned it.

❖

An upbeat! An upbeat!
–Alban Berg
COMPOSER

❖

An enemy soldier stepped on mathmetician Archimedes'
geometry drawings in the sand. Archimedes responded:
MAN, DO NOT DISTURB MY FIGURES.

❖

Let me hear those notes so long my solace and delight.
–Wolfgang Amadeus Mozart
COMPOSER

Dictionary.
–Joseph Wright
LINGUIST

✣

A thousand greetings to Balakirev.
–Hector Berlioz
COMPOSER

✣

France! Army! Head of the Army! Josephine!
–Napoleon I
EMPEROR OF THE FRENCH AND KING OF ITALY

✣

U.S. President John F. Kennedy was firm about visiting Dallas:
IF SOMEONE IS GOING TO KILL ME, THEY WILL KILL ME.

✣

Politician Benjamin Disraeli was correcting the proofs of his last Parliamentary speech:
I will not go down to posterity talking bad grammar.

Broadway Producer Florenz Ziegfeld remembered the excitement of opening night:

CURTAIN!
FAST MUSIC!
LIGHT!
READY FOR THE LAST FINALE!
GREAT!
THE SHOW LOOKS GOOD,
THE SHOW LOOKS GOOD!

❖

WHAT'S THE NEWS?
–Clarence W. Barron
NEWSPAPER PUBLISHER

❖

Get my "Swan" costume ready.
–Anna Pavlova
DANCER

Everyday Matters

Have you brought the check-book, Alfred?
—Samuel Butler
WRITER

✢

I should like to have a good spin down Regent Street.
—Robert Buchanan
WRITER

✢

Telegram.
—Alfred Nobel
CHEMIST

✢

U.S. President Thomas Jefferson died on July 4, 1826, the 50th anniversary
of the ratification of the Declaration of Independence.
He died five hours before John Adams. Jefferson's last words were:

IS IT THE FOURTH?

Poet E. E. Cummings was chopping wood on a hot day:
I'm going to stop now, but I'm going to sharpen the axe
before I put it up, dear.

✛

*Lyricist Oscar Hammerstein II mentioned the names of his
favorite baseball players:*
RUTH . . . GEHRIG . . . RIZZUTO . . .

✛

IS IT NOT MENINGITIS?
–Louisa May Alcott
WRITER

✛

TODAY I LEARNED SOMETHING!
–Pierre-Auguste Renoir
ARTIST

✛

The clock must be wound tomorrow.
–Charles II
KING OF ENGLAND

Philosophical Thoughts

Life, life! Death, death! How curious it is!
–Daniel Webster
POLITICIAN

✣

I have not yet lost my feeling for humanity.
–Immanuel Kant
PHILOSOPHER

✣

EVER PRECIOUS, EVER PRECIOUS.
–Joseph Duncan
POLITICIAN

✣

I don't know what I may seem to the world. But as to
myself, I seem to have been only a boy playing on the seashore
and diverting myself in now and then finding a smoother pebble
or prettier shell than the ordinary, whilst the great ocean of
truth lay all undiscovered before me.
–Isaac Newton
PHYSICIST

WHAT A BOON IT WOULD BE, IF
WHEN LIFE DRAWS TO ITS CLOSE,
ONE COULD PASS AWAY WITHOUT
A STRUGGLE.
–Nathaniel Hawthorne
WRITER

✛

The world is bobbing around.
–Sam Bass
OUTLAW

✛

**THE ISSUE NOW IS CLEAR:
IT IS BETWEEN LIGHT AND DARKNESS
AND EVERYONE MUST CHOOSE HIS SIDE.**
–G. K. Chesterton
WRITER

✛

SO THIS IS HOW THEY LET YOU DIE.
–Coco Chanel
FASHION DESIGNER

Does nobody understand?
—James Joyce
WRITER

✤

This was Amelia Earhart's last letter to her husband:
Please know that I am quite aware of the hazards.
I want to do it because I want to do it. Women must try to do things as men have tried. When they fail, their failure must be but a challenge to others.
—Amelia Earhart
AVIATOR

✤

LOVE, LOVE, LOVE!
—Norman Douglas
WRITER

✤

WHAT WE KNOW IS NOT MUCH, WHAT WE DO NOT KNOW IS IMMENSE.
—Pierre-Simon Laplace
ASTRONOMER

The Beauty of the Earth

Below my window . . . the blossom is out in full now . . . I *see* it is the whitest, frothiest, bloomiest blossom that there ever could be, and I can see it. Things are both more trivial than they ever were, and more important than they ever were, and the difference between the trivial and the important doesn't seem to matter. But the nowness of everything is absolutely wondrous.

—Dennis Potter
WRITER

✢

It is very beautiful over there.
—Thomas Edison
INVENTOR

✢

HELP ME GET OUT OF BED.
I WANT TO LOOK AT THE SUNSET.
—Carl Jung
PSYCHIATRIST

✢

Abolitionist John Brown spoke these words as he went to the gallows:
This *is* a beautiful country.

I love to see the reflection of the sun on the bookcase.
–Marion Crawford
WRITER

✣

Raise my bed, so I can look out the window and see my studio.
–Walt Disney
FILM PRODUCER

✣

What a beautiful day!
–Alexander I
EMPEROR OF RUSSIA

✣

Oh look, see how the cherry blossoms fall mutely.
–Hideki Tojo
PRIME MINISTER OF JAPAN

✣

DON'T PULL DOWN THE BLINDS.
I FEEL FINE.
I WANT THE SUNLIGHT TO GREET ME!
–Rudolph Valentino
ACTOR

I Did My Best

That was a great game of golf, fellers.
–Bing Crosby
SINGER

✦

LIFE IS WONDERFUL . . . I AM WONDERFUL . . .
–Mary McLeod Bethune
EDUCATOR

✦

First Lady of Argentina Eva Perón's last words were to her maid:
I have never felt happy in this life. That's why I left home.
My mother would have married me to someone ordinary
and I could never have stood it. Irma, a decent woman has
to get on in the world.

✦

I have enjoyed a world which, though wicked enough
in all conscience, is perhaps as good as worlds unknown.
–John James Audubon
ORNITHOLOGIST

John Wilkes Booth, the assasin of U.S. President Abraham Lincoln,
uttered these famous last words:
Tell my mother I died for my country.
I did what I thought was for the best. Useless. Useless.

❖

I have tried so hard to do right.
–Grover Cleveland
U.S. PRESIDENT

❖

WITH THE BEST THAT WAS IN ME
I HAVE TRIED TO WRITE MORE
HAPPINESS INTO THE WORLD.
–Frances Hodgson Burnett
WRITER

More Time, Please

*Clergyman Stopford Augustus Brooke said the following words
on hearing the newspaper read to him:*
It will be a pity to leave all that.

❖

Oh that peace may come. Bertie!
–Victoria
QUEEN OF THE UNITED KINGDOM

❖

*Composer Béla Bartók was disappointed that he wouldn't
get to finish his piano concerto:*
I am only sad that I have to leave with a full trunk.

❖

**LET ME DIE IN MY OLD UNIFORM.
GOD FORGIVE ME FOR EVER
HAVING PUT ON ANOTHER.
–Benedict Arnold**
CONTINENTAL ARMY GENERAL (AND TRAITOR) DURING
THE AMERICAN REVOLUTION

I am not the least afraid to die. I am only sorry that
I haven't the strength to go on with my research.
–Charles Darwin
NATURALIST

❖

This was writer William Saroyan's last phone call to the Associated Press:
Everybody has got to die, but I always believed
an exception would be made in my case. Now what?

❖

I HAVE ONLY TWO REGRETS–
THAT I HAVE NOT SHOT HENRY CLAY
OR HANGED JOHN C. CALHOUN.
–Andrew Jackson
U.S. PRESIDENT

❖

Don't let it end like this. Tell them I said something.
–Pancho Villa
GENERAL DURING THE MEXICAN REVOLUTION

I Need a Rest . . . and a Drink!

I MUST SLEEP NOW.
–George Byron
POET

❖

Softly, quite softly.
–Joseph Pulitzer
NEWSPAPER PUBLISHER

❖

PUT OUT THE LIGHT.
–Theodore Roosevelt
U.S. PRESIDENT

❖

I can't sleep.
–J. M. Barrie
WRITER

❖

Take away those pillows—I shall need them no more.
–Lewis Carroll
WRITER

I want to be quiet.
–Thomas Cole
ARTIST

✛

I'M BORED.
–James Baldwin
WRITER

✛

Physicist and chemist Marie Curie refused an injection from the nurse:
I DON'T WANT IT. I WANT TO
BE LEFT ALONE.

✛

Writer F. Scott Fitzgerald's last request was for Hershey Bars:
Good enough, they'll be fine.

✛

Physicist Albert Einstein's last words were to his son:
YOUR PRESENCE WON'T STOP ME
FROM GOING TO SLEEP.

Social worker Jane Addams refused to take spirits:
ALWAYS, ALWAYS WATER FOR ME!

✛

Composer Johannes Brahms sipped his last glass of wine:
AH, THAT TASTES NICE. THANK YOU.

✛

It has been some time since I have drunk champagne.
—Anton Chekhov
WRITER

✛

DRINK TO ME.
—Pablo Picasso
ARTIST

Courageous Until the End

Give them the cold steel, boys.
–Lewis Addison Armistead
CONFEDERATE BRIGADIER GENERAL DURING THE U.S. CIVIL WAR

✛

I could wish this tragic scene were over,
but I hope to go through it with becoming modesty.
–James Quin
ACTOR

✛

By gad, I'm not licked yet.
–Elias Jackson Baldwin
GAMBLER

✛

Men, it is good for me to die on this spot,
where honour bids me; but you hurry and save yourselves
before the enemy can close with us.
–Anaxibius
SPARTAN ADMIRAL

Let me go! Let me go!
–Clara Barton
FOUNDER OF THE AMERICAN RED CROSS

✛

I strike my flag.
–Isaac Hull
COMMODORE IN THE U.S. NAVY

✛

Don't give me anything. None of those anodynes to dull the senses or relieve pain. I want to feel it all. And—please tell me when the time is near. I want to know.
–Dorothea Dix
ACTIVIST

✛

I WILL THROW UP MY HANDS FOR NO GRINGO DOG.
–Three Fingered Jack
OUTLAW

✛

So here it is at last, the distinguished thing!
–Henry James
WRITER

*Composer Edvard Grieg was told that he probably wouldn't
survive his heart attack. He responded:*
Well, if it must be so.

✤

I DON'T WANT TO DIE WITH MY BOOTS ON!
–Billy Clanton
COWBOY

✤

I only regret that I have but one life to lose for my country.
–Nathan Hale
CONTINENTAL ARMY CAPTAIN DURING THE AMERICAN REVOLUTION

✤

TAKING A LEAP INTO THE DARK.
O MYSTERY!
–Thomas Paine
WRITER

✤

Writer Marie Bashkirtseff addressed the candle by her bed:
We shall go out together.

A Surprise Interruption

*A Confederate North Carolina regiment mistook Confederate General
Stonewall Jackson's troops for a Union cavalry and shot Jackson.
He responded:*

LET US CROSS OVER THE RIVER AND
SIT IN THE SHADE OF THE TREES.

❖

*Composer Franz Liszt collapsed at a performance
of Wagner's Tristan and Isolde:*

TRISTAN!

❖

*Dancer Josephine Baker wanted to continue partying
but was taken back to her apartment:*

OH, YOU YOUNG PEOPLE ACT LIKE
OLD MEN, YOU ARE NOT FUN!

❖

HERE . . .
–Joseph Conrad
WRITER

Outlaw Billy the Kid spoke his last words to his killer, Pat Garrett:

WHO IS THERE?

❖

What's this?
–Leonard Bernstein
COMPOSER

❖

Outlaw Jesse James was shot by Bob Ford and said:

IF ANY BODY PASSES, THEY'LL SEE ME.
–Jesse James
OUTLAW

Good-byes

A general good-night.
–Thomas Chalmers
CLERGYMAN

❖

Writer Herman Melville quoted his character Billy Budd's last words:
GOD BLESS CAPTAIN VERE!

❖

*Actor Marilyn Monroe's last conversation was on the phone
with actor and Kennedy in-law, Peter Lawford:*
Say good-bye to Pat, say good-bye to the president, and say good-bye
to yourself, because you're a nice guy . . . I'll see . . . I'll see . . . .

❖

Singer Elvis Presley's last words were to his female companion:
PRECIOUS, I'M GOING TO GO
INTO THE BATHROOM AND READ.

Queen of France, Marie Antoinette accidentally tripped over the executioner's foot:
Excuse me, sir; I did not do it on purpose.

✠

*Writer Ernest Hemingway said these words to his wife
on the night before he committed suicide:*
Goodnight, my kitten.

✠

*U.S. President Ronald Reagan wrote these words in a farewell letter to the
American people in 1994. He announced that he had been diagnosed
with Alzheimer's disease:*
I NOW BEGIN THE JOURNEY THAT WILL
LEAD ME INTO THE SUNSET OF MY LIFE.
I KNOW THAT FOR AMERICA THERE
WILL ALWAYS BE A BRIGHT DAWN AHEAD.

✠

*Actor Humphrey Bogart said good-bye to his wife, Lauren Bacall,
before she went to pick up their children from Sunday school:*
GOOD-BYE, KID. HURRY BACK.

Last Words for Friends and Loved Ones

Take courage Charlotte, take courage.
–Anne Brontë
WRITER

�֍

God bless you.
–William Wordsworth
POET

✖

Writer Miguel de Cervantes wrote the following words:
Goodbye, all that is charming. Goodbye, wit and gaiety.
Goodbye, merry friends, for I am dying and wish
to see you contented in another life.

✖

Actor Cary Grant's last words were to his wife:
I love you, Barbara. Don't worry.

✖

Prince Albert of Saxe-Coburg and Gotha said this of Queen Victoria:
GOOD LITTLE WOMAN.

Writer Charlotte Brontë's last words were to her husband:
Oh, I'm not going to die, am I? He would not separate us.
We have been so happy.

❈

Actor Rex Harrison's last words were to his wife:
WHAT DID I DO TO DESERVE YOU?

❈

Actor Bette Davis mentioned her estranged daughter:
Tell B. D. I'm sorry. I loved her. I really did love her.

❈

Writer Ralph Waldo Emerson's last words were to his friend, Amos Bronson Alcott:
GOOD-BYE, MY FRIEND.

❈

Writer L. Frank Baum whispered to his wife about the Shifting Sands,
the boundary between Oz and this world:
NOW WE CAN CROSS
THE SHIFTING SANDS.

Educator Anthony Benezet's last words were to his wife:
WE HAVE LIVED LONG, IN LOVE AND PEACE.

✤

There ought to be a medal struck for you, inscribed,
"To the best of all nurses."
—Arthur Conan Doyle
WRITER

✤

Thomas Jefferson still survives.
—John Adams
U.S. PRESIDENT

✤

Writer Mary Wollstonecraft's last words were about her husband:
He is the kindest, best man in the world.

✤

Philosopher Jean-Paul Sartre's last words were to his companion, Simone de Beauvoir:
I love you very much, my dear Beaver.

Carry On for Me

Mayor of Chicago Anton Cermak was wounded in the abdomen, a shot that was intended for president-elect Franklin D. Roosevelt

I'M GLAD IT WAS ME INSTEAD OF YOU, FRANK. THE COUNTRY NEEDS YOU.

❖

Queen Anne of Great Britain handed the white staff of the Lord Treasurer to the Duke of Shrewsbury:

USE IT FOR THE GOOD OF MY PEOPLE.

❖

Bury me where the birds will sing over my grave.
—Alexander Wilson
ORNITHOLOGIST

❖

The South! The South! God knows what will become of her.
—John C. Calhoun
POLITICIAN

Give the boys a holiday.
—Anaxagoras
PHILOSOPHER

✣

QUICK! SERVE THE DESSERT!
I THINK I AM DYING.
—Paulette Brillat-Savarin
SISTER OF JEAN ANTHELME BRILLAT-SAVARIN, THE FRENCH EPICURE

✣

Make the world better!
—Lucy Stone
SUFFRAGIST

✣

When asked to whom he wished to leave the throne,
Alexander the Great, King of Macedon, replied:
TO THE STRONGEST.

I'm Going Home

I see the black light!
—Victor Hugo
WRITER

✤

I am seeing things that you know nothing of.
—William Allingham
POET

✤

Composer Sergei Rachmaninoff asked his wife if she heard the ethereal music.
She said that there was no one playing. He responded:
WHO IS IT THAT KEEPS PLAYING? . . .
A-AH! THAT MEANS IT'S PLAYING
IN MY HEAD.

✤

I believe we must adjourn the meeting to some other place.
—Adam Smith
ECONOMIST

Stepping out into the light, oh, won't that be glorious?
Oh, I'm not going to die! I'm just going home like a shooting star!

–Sojourner Truth

ABOLITIONIST

❖

Do not grieve, my friend, my dearest friend. I am ready to go.
And John, it will not be long.

–Abigail Adams

U.S. FIRST LADY

❖

It's very beautiful, but I want to go farther away.

–Augustus Saint-Gaudens

ARTIST

❖

Waiting God's Leave to die.

–Isaac Watts

HYMN WRITER

❖

Do you hear the music? Now I go hence.

–Jakob Böhme

CHRISTIAN MYSTIC

When you come to the hedge we must all go over, it isn't so bad.
You feel sleepy and you don't care. Just a little dreamy anxiety . . .
which world you're really in . . . that's all . . .
–Stephen Crane
WRITER

✣

**THE ROAD TO HEAVEN
IS AS SHORT BY SEA AS BY LAND.**
–Humphrey Gilbert
EXPLORER

✣

Poet William Blake's wife asked him about the songs that he was singing:
My beloved, they are not mine, no, they are not mine.

✣

I shall hear in heaven!
–Ludwig van Beethoven
COMPOSER

✣

NOW I WANT TO GO HOME.
–Vincent van Gogh
ARTIST

Witty Remarks

If God wants another joke man, I'm ready.
–Jackie Gleason
ACTOR

✛

All right, then, I'll say it: Dante makes me sick.
–Lope de Vega
WRITER

✛

MY EXIT IS THE RESULT
OF TOO MANY ENTRÉES.
–Richard Monckton Milnes
POET

✛

The executioner is, I hear, very expert,
and my neck is very slender.
–Anne Boleyn
SECOND WIFE OF HENRY VIII OF GREAT BRITAIN

I can feel the daisies growing over me.
–John Keats
POET

✜

Better burn the writer than his work!
–Hilaire Belloc
WRITER

✜

Catharina Goethe, mother of poet Johann Wolfgang Goethe, declined an invitation to a party:
Say that Frau Goethe is unable to come,
she is busy dying at the moment.

✜

**MY WALLPAPER AND I
ARE FIGHTING A DUEL TO THE DEATH.
ONE OR THE OTHER OF US HAS TO GO.**
–Oscar Wilde
WRITER

A Happy Ending

And my heart throbbed with an exquisite bliss.
—William Makepeace Thackeray
WRITER

✥

HAPPY.
—Raphael
ARTIST

I am resting. This rest is more magnificent,
more beautiful than words can tell.
—John Ericsson
INVENTOR

✥

I love everybody. If ever I had an enemy
I should hope to meet and welcome that enemy in heaven.
—Christina Rossetti
POET

✥

BEAUTIFUL.
—Elizabeth Barrett Browning
POET

Writer H. G. Wells' last words were to his nurse:
GO AWAY. I'M ALL RIGHT.

✤

My horizon has cleared. My thoughts are tinged
with sweetness and I am content.
–Bruce Cummings
BIOLOGIST

✤

IS EVERYBODY HAPPY?
I WANT EVERYBODY TO BE HAPPY.
I KNOW I'M HAPPY.
–Ethel Barrymore
ACTOR

✤

To those who ask how Isaac Pitman passed away,
say peacefully and with no more concern than passing from
one room into another to take up some further employment.
–Isaac Pitman
INVENTOR OF PITMAN SHORTHAND

*Poet Robert Browning received a telegram about the popularity
of his volume of poems,* Asolando. *He responded:*

HOW GRATIFYING.

✛

HAPPY, HAPPY, SUPREMELY HAPPY.
–John Copley
ARTIST

✛

This is the last of earth. I am content.
–John Quincy Adams
U.S. PRESIDENT

✛

*After U.S. President George Washington gave Tobias Lear his burial
instructions he asked if that was understood. Lear said yes.
Then Washington replied with the following:*

'TIS WELL.

Index

A

Ackerman, Diane, 99
Adams, Abigail, 149
Adams, John, 37, 122, 145
Adams, John Quincy, 155
Adams, Julie, 57
Adams, Samuel, 31
Addams, Jane, 135
Ade, George, 78
Alcott, Amos Bronson, 144
Alcott, Louisa May, 123
Alexander I, 128
Alexander the Great, 28, 73, 147
Allen, Fred, 76, 80
Allen, Gracie, 23
Allen, Woody, 106, 110
Allingham, William, 148
Anaxagoras, 147
Anaxibius, 136
Andersen, Hans Christian, 81
Antoinette, Marie, 141
Archimedes, 119
Armistead, Lewis Addison, 136
Armstrong, Louis, 20
Arnold, Benedict, 131
Ashe, Arthur, 43
Ashman, Howard, 13
Asimov, Isaac, 101
Astaire, Fred, 14
Atwood, Eliza, 57
Atwood, Mary, 57
Atwood, Sarah, 57
Auden, W. H., 60
Audubon, John James, 129
Austen, Jane, 63, 98
Austin, Stephen F., 118

B

Bacall, Lauren, 142
Bacon, Francis, 116
Baker, Josephine, 139
Baker, Russell, 70, 96
Balanchine, George, 9
Baldwin, Elias Jackson, 136
Baldwin, James, 134
Balzac, Honor de, 118
Barford, Susanna, 47
Barnum, P. T., 83, 118
Barrie, J. M., 133
Barron, Clarence W., 121
Barrymore, Ethel, 154
Barrymore, Lionel, 20
Bartók, Béla, 131
Barton, Clara, 137
Bashkirtseff, Marie, 138
Bass, Sam, 125
Baum, L. Frank, 144
Beauvoir, Simone de, 145
Beethoven, Ludwig van, 150
Behan, Brendan Francis, 72
Behrman, S. N., 71
Belloc, Hilaire, 152
Benchley, Robert, 24, 61
Benezet, Anthony, 145
Bennett, Alan, 72
Benny, Jack, 11
Bent, Mary Ann, 45
Bentley, Nicolas, 29
Berg, Alban, 119
Bergman, Ingrid, 117
Berlioz, Hector, 120
Bernstein, Leonard, 140
Bethune, Mary McLeod, 129
Bierce, Ambrose, 86, 89
Bill (mule), 52
Billings, Josh, 110
Billy the Kid, 36, 140
Bird, Nodiah, 41
Black, Jonathan, 56
Blake, William, 150
Blanc, Mel, 23
Bloomfield, Ernest, 40

Boatswain (dog), 53
Bogart, Humphrey, 142
Böhme, Jakob, 149
Boleyn, Anne, 151
Bombeck, Erma, 64
Bonney, William H., 36, 140
Bono, Sonny, 12
Bonzo (chimpanzee), 49
Booth, John Wilkes, 130
Boutelle, Charles A., 76
Bowker, Charles, 56
Bowra, Maurice, 95
Boyd, William, 51
Bradbury, Thomas, 40
Bradbury, William, 40
Bradley, Francis Herbert, 69
Brahms, Johannes, 135
Brailey, W. Theodore, 12
Bricous, Roger, 12
Brillat-Savarin, Paulette, 147
Brisbane, Arthur, 88
Brontë, Anne, 143
Brontë, Charlotte, 144
Brooke, Stopford Augustus, 131
Brooks, Louise, 13
Broomfield, Mary, 59
Brown, David McDowell, 31
Brown, John, 127
Browning, Elizabeth Barrett, 153
Browning, Robert, 155
Bruce, Lenny, 19
Bruns, Joshua, 112
Brussell, Eugene E., 88
Brynner, Yul, 119
Buchanan, Robert, 122
Burbage, Richard, 10
Burgess, Anthony, 68
Burnett, Frances Hodgson, 130
Burns, George, 23, 108, 112
Burns, John, 24

Burr, Aaron, 35
Burroughs, William S., 61
Butler, Nicholas Murray, 101
Butler, Samuel, 94, 103, 122
Button, 45
Byron, George, 53, 133

C

Caine, Michael, 18
Calculator (dog), 52
Calhoun, John C., 146
Cameron, James, 97
Camp, Walter, 42
Campan, Jeanne-Louise-
   Henriette, 117
Campbell-Bannerman, Henry,
   29
Capone, Al, 29
Capote, Truman, 95
Carpenter, Karen, 22
Carroll, Lewis, 133
Carson, Johnny, 13, 91
Cash, Johnny, 9
Cash, June Carter, 9
Cato the Elder, 87
Céline, Louis-Ferdinand, 72
Cermak, Anton, 146
Cervantes, Miguel de, 143
Chalmers, Thomas, 141
Chanel, Coco, 125
Charles II, 123
Charles, Ray, 108
Chekhov, Anton, 135
Chesterton, G. K., 125
Churchill, Winston, 109
Clanton, Billy, 138
Clark, John Frederick
   Preston, 12
Clark, William, 37
Clemens, James Ross, 95
Cleveland, Grover, 130
Cobb, Irvin S., 84

Cohn, Harry, 77
Cole, Thomas, 134
Connor, William, 98
Conrad, Joseph, 139
Cooke, Jay, 116
Cooley, Mason, 68, 105, 109
Coolidge, Calvin, 97
Cooper, Henry Hughes, 47
Copenhagen (horse), 49
Copley, John, 155
Coward, Noël, 66, 80, 83, 84,
   111
Crane, Stephen, 150
Crawford, Marion, 128
Crosby, Bing, 10, 129
Cummings, Bruce, 154
Cummings, E. E., 31, 123
Curie, Marie, 134
Cushman, Mary, 33

D

da Vinci, Leonardo, 102
D'Amato, Constantine, 43
Dangerfield, Rodney, 16
Darden, Severn, 109
Darrow, Clarence, 83
Darwin, Charles, 132
Davis, Bette, 21, 144
Davis, Sammy, Jr., 18
Davis, Thomas, 64
Day, James Edward, 91
de Gaulle, Charles, 89
Dempsey, Jack, 44
DeRita, Joe, 17
Dickinson, Emily, 66, 114
Dillingham, Charles B., 96
DiMaggio, Joe, 42
Disney, Walt, 128
Disraeli, Benjamin, 120
Dix, Dorothea, 137
Donleavy, J. P., 106
Donne, John, 104

Dorsey, Thomas, Jr., 22
Douglas, Norman, 126
Doyle, Arthur Conan, 145
Duke of Shrewsbury, 146
Duke of Wellington, 49
Duncan, Joseph, 124
Durante, Jimmy, 92
Durrell, Lawrence, 71
Dyer, Wayne, 102

E

Earhart, Amelia, 38, 126
Earl of Kildare, 57
Earp, Wyatt, 32
Edison, Thomas, 127
Edwards, John, 40
Einstein, Albert, 100, 134
Eisenhower, Dwight, 98
Ellington, Duke, 15, 104
Emerson, Ralph Waldo, 144
Ensign, Susannah, 45
Ericsson, John, 153
Evans, Edith, 69

F

Fairbanks, Douglas, 21
Fields, W. C., 8
Fitzgerald, F. Scott, 134
Folkestone, Rebeca Bogess,
   47
Ford, Bob, 140
Ford, Wallace, 23
Foster, Vince, 77
Fox, Henry, 111
Franklin, Benjamin, 94
Frederick, Prince of Wales, 33
Frisch, Max, 71
Fuller, Thomas, 87

G

Gable, Clark, 80
Garfield, John, 18
Garrett, Pat, 140
Gaylord, Milla, 54
General (horse), 50
Gilbert, Humphrey, 150
Gilbert, W. S., 8
Gilman, Irv, 82
Gleason, Jackie, 151
Goethe, Catharina, 152
Goethe, Johann Wolfgang, 152
Gold, Mary, 25
Goldwyn, Samuel, 100
Gordon, Barbara, 100
Gottfried von Herder, Johann, 117
Graham, Billy, 93
Grandma Moses, 102
Grant, Cary, 19, 109, 143
Grieg, Edvard, 138
Groombridge, Richard, 26
Grylls, David, 90

H

Hale, Nathan, 138
Hamilton, Alexander, 30
Hammerstein, Oscar, II, 123
Handel, George Frederick, 11
Harding, Warren G., 31, 117
Hardy, Oliver, 16
Hardy, Thomas, 62
Harrison, Rex, 144
Hartley, William Henry, 12
Hawthorne, Nathaniel, 108, 125
Hayworth, Rita, 21
Hemingway, Ernest, 64, 142
Hendrix, Jimi, 11, 90
Henry, Patrick, 28

Henry VIII, 119
Hepburn, Katharine, 90
Herbert, Mary, 58
Herold, Don, 70
Hind, Richard, 24
Hitchcock, Alfred, 9
Hobhouse, John Cam, 53
Hoffa, Jimmy, 97
Holiday, Billie, 10
Holliday, Doc, 36
Holmes, Oliver Wendell, Sr., 107
Hopalong Cassidy, 51
Houdini, Harry, 96
Houseman, A. E., 105
Howe, Edgar Watson, 90
Hubbard, Elbert, 74, 85
Huddlestone, Thomas, 59
Hugo, Victor, 148
Hull, Isaac, 137
Hume, Benita, 111
Hume, John Law, 12
Hurley, Jack, 77

I

Irving, Washington, 78, 86
Ives, Burl, 14

J

Jackson, Andrew, 132
Jackson, Stonewall, 139
James, Henry, 60, 137
James, Jesse, 140
James, John, 54
Jefferson, Thomas, 27, 122, 145
Jessel, George, 23
Johnson, Samuel, 86, 107, 117
Jones, George, 56
Jones, Jemima, 55
Joplin, Janis, 98

Joyce, James, 126
Jung, Carl, 127

K

Kahlo, Frida, 108
Kant, Immanuel, 124
Kaufman, George S., 60
Kaye, Danny, 99
Keats, John, 152
Keillor, Garrison, 82
Keller, Helen, 103
Kennedy, John F., 120
King, Coretta Scott, 34
King, Martin Luther, Jr., 38
Krins, George, 12
Krutch, Joseph Wood, 76
Kübler-Ross, Elisabeth, 104

L

Lamarr, Hedy, 17
Lamb, Charles, 81, 85
Landers, Ann, 92
Lantz, Gracie, 46
Lantz, Walter, 46
Laplace, Pierre-Simon, 126
Laurel, Stan, 18
Lawford, Peter, 141
Lawrence, D. H., 61
Lawrence, Gertrude, 80, 119
Lawrence, T. E., 32
La-Zi-Yah, 30
Lear, Tobias, 155
Leary, Timothy, 114
Lee, Bruce, 42
Leigh, Vivien, 15
Lemmon, Jack, 92
Leonard, Elmore, 75
Levenson, Sam, 110
Levinson, Leonard L., 79
Lewis, C. S., 65, 114
Liberace, 22

Liddell, Eric, 44
Lincoln, Abraham, 34, 130
Lindbergh, Charles, 28
Liszt, Franz, 139
Little, Mary Wilson, 85
Low, David, 46
Lynd, Robert, 93

M

Maggie (mule), 51
Magranis, Francis, 48
Major (dog), 49
Mansfield, Jane, 16
Mansfield, Katherine, 101, 116
Mantle, Mickey, 44
Marquis, Don, 93
Marshall, Arthur, 81
Martin, Dean, 19
Martin, Edward Sanford, 88
Marx, Karl, 29
Maugham, W. Somerset, 68
McAuliffe, Christa, 35
Melville, Herman, 141
Mencken, H. L., 105
Mercer, Johnny, 8
Merterlinck, Maurice, 92
Miller, Arthur, 78
Milnes, Richard Monckton, 151
Mitford, Jessica, 75
Moldea, Don E., 97
Monroe, Marilyn, 78, 141
Montaigne, Michel de, 69
Mozart, Wolfgang Amadeus, 119

N

Napoleon I, 97, 120
Newton, Isaac, 124
Nin, Anaïs, 101

Nisker, Wes "Scoop," 99
Nobel, Alfred, 122

O

O'Day, Mike, 58
O'Rourke, P. J., 81, 111, 112

P

Paine, Thomas, 65, 138
Parker, Dorothy, 66, 91, 97
Parks, Rosa, 28
Pavlova, Anna, 121
Pell, Claiborne, 75
Penn, William, 104
Perón, Eva, 129
Phelps, Michael, 107
Phillips, John, 39
Picasso, Pablo, 135
Pitman, Isaac, 154
Plunkitt, George W., 34
Porter, Katherine Anne, 73
Potter, Dennis, 127
Presley, Elvis, 141
Prince Albert, 143
Print (dog), 50
Pritchard, Michael, 77
Pulitzer, Joseph, 133

Q

Queen Anne, 146
Queen Victoria, 131, 143
Quin, James, 136

R

Rabelais, François, 115
Rachmaninoff, Sergei, 148
Radner, Gilda, 22
Raphael, 153

Rastas (monkey), 52
Reagan, Ronald, 38, 49, 142
Reisner, Robert, 107
Renoir, Pierre-Auguste, 123
Reston, James, 70
Richardson, Ralph, 79
Robeson, Paul, 20
Robinson, Jackie, 42
Rogers, Will, 106
Rooney, Andy, 106
Roosevelt, Franklin D., 103, 146
Roosevelt, Theodore, 133
Rosa (cow), 50
Rossetti, Christina, 153
Rousseau, Jean-Jacques, 115
Roy, Rob, 116
Russell, William Howard, 61
Ruth, Babe, 43

S

Sahl, Mort, 105
Saint-Gaudens, Augustus, 149
Saroyan, William, 132
Sartre, Jean-Paul, 145
Sayers, Dorothy L., 96
Schubert, Franz, 114
Schulz, Charles M., 46
Schweitzer, Albert, 36
Scott, Johnnie, 25
Shakespeare, William, 66
Shaw, Bernard, 100
Shaw, George Bernard, 78
Shore, Dinah, 19
Shore, Jane, 55
Sinatra, Frank, 8
Sinclair, Upton, 61
Skelton, Red, 77
Sloan, John, 91
Smith, Adam, 148
Smith, Horace, 69
Smith, Logan Pearsall, 111

Smith, Stevie, 99
Smith, Sydney, 103
Spellman, Cardinal, 43
Stalin, Joseph, 98
Stanhope, Philip Dormer, 82
Steinem, Gloria, 102
Stengel, Casey, 44
Stewart, Jimmy, 13
Stone, I. F., 79
Stone, Lucy, 147
Strachey, Lytton, 70
Swanson, Gloria, 17

T

Taylor, Percy Cornelius, 12
Taylor, Zachary, 115
Thackeray, William
  Makepeace, 153
Thomas, Gwyn, 77
Thoreau, Henry David, 84
Three Fingered Jack, 137
Tojo, Hideki, 128
Topper (horse), 51
Travers, Ben, 62
Truth, Sojourner, 149
Turner, Ted, 17
Twain, Mark, 71, 78, 89, 95
Twynnoy, Hannah, 58
Tyler, John, 50, 115

V

Valentino, Rudolph, 128
van Gogh, Vincent, 150
Vega, Lope de, 151
Vidal, Gore, 95
Villa, Pancho, 132
von Haller, Albrecht, 115

W

Wallace, Lew, 87
Warhol, Andy, 92, 110
Washington, George, 155
Watts, Isaac, 149
Wayne, John, 15
Webster, Daniel, 124
Welk, Lawrence, 17
Wells, H. G., 62, 154
Wheldon, Huw, 64
Whitman, Alden, 93
Wilde, Oscar, 73, 152
Wilder, Billy, 60
Williams, Robin, 68
Wilson, Alexander, 146
Wilson, Carl Dean, 16
Wilson, Woodrow, 116
Wollstonecraft, Mary, 145
Woodward, John Wesley, 12
Wordsworth, William, 143
Wright, Joseph, 120
Wright, Steven, 79, 108

Y

Yates, Douglas, 79
Yeats, William Butler, 60
Youngman, Henry, 94
Ysaÿe, Eugène, 118

Z

Ziegfeld, Florenz, 121